LIBRARY OF RELIGIOUS BIOGRAPHY

Edited by Mark A. Noll, Nathan O. Hatch, and Allen C. Guelzo

THE LIBRARY OF RELIGIOUS BIOGRAPHY is a series of original biographies on important religious figures throughout American and British history.

The authors are well-known historians, each a recognized authority in the period of religious history in which his or her subject lived and worked. Grounded in solid research of both published and archival sources, these volumes link the lives of their subjects — not always thought of as "religious" persons — to the broader cultural contexts and religious issues that surrounded them. This volume includes a bibliographical essay and an index to serve the needs of students, teachers, and researchers.

Marked by careful scholarship yet free of footnotes and academic jargon, the books in this series are well-written narratives meant to be *read* and *enjoyed* as well as studied.

LIBRARY OF RELIGIOUS BIOGRAPHY

A SHORT LIFE OF
JONATHAN EDWARDS

George M. Marsden

WILLIAM B. EERDMANS PUBLISHING COMPANY
GRAND RAPIDS, MICHIGAN / CAMBRIDGE, U.K.

Published 2008 by

Wm. B. Eerdmans Publishing Co.

2140 Oak Industrial Drive N.E., Grand Rapids, Michigan 49505 /

P.O. Box 163, Cambridge CB3 9PU U.K.

Printed in the United States of America

13 12   7 6 5 4 3

Library of Congress Cataloging-in-Publication Data

Marsden, George M., 1939-

A short life of Jonathan Edwards / George M. Marsden.

p.   cm.   — (Library of religious biography)

ISBN 978-0-8028-0220-0 (pbk.: alk. paper)

1. Edwards, Jonathan, 1703-1758.

2. Congregational churches — United States —

Clergy — Biography.   I. Title.

BX7260.E3M415   2008

285.8092 — dc22

[B]

2008012433

www.eerdmans.com

For
Anneke, Zach, Saskia,
Elena, and Vivian

Contents

—∞∞∞—

vii

Preface

—◦◦◦—

My hope is that this brief biography will make Jonathan Edwards accessible to a wide variety of readers. Edwards is, by all accounts, one of the most remarkable figures in American history. More broadly, he is one of the most influential and respected Americans in the history of Christianity. Yet he is not as well known or understood as he should be. Most people who know anything about him recall only something about a school assignment of his sermon "Sinners in the Hands of an Angry God," which has left them with a stereotyped impression at best. I hope that this book will provide the general reader with a view that is more balanced at the same time it is entertaining, informative, and short.

The origins of this book help explain its character. In 2003 I published *Jonathan Edwards: A Life* with Yale University Press on the occasion of the three-hundredth anniversary of Edwards's birth. Prior to being asked to write that major biography, I had already told my friends at Eerdmans that some day I would write a life of Edwards for them. So with the cooperation of both publishers, I agreed that after I wrote the more definitive biography for Yale, I would write something shorter for Eerdmans. The happy outcome is that, having already published a much longer, closely documented work, this book could be kept brief without any scholarly apparatus. With the exception of a few items noted in the acknowledgments, documentation for whatever is said here can be found in the larger work. Nevertheless, I need to emphasize that this book is not an abridgement of *Jonathan Edwards: A Life*. Rather it is a fresh retelling in which I have tried to include just what is most essential and most engaging. A few things, especially the recurrent theme of Edwards and Franklin, are new. My hope is that the result will appeal not only to the general reader but also to church study groups and to students in college courses in American history or American religious history. In the retelling, I have tried to keep the interests of each of these audiences in mind.

Acknowledgments

—⌘—

This book, like *Jonathan Edwards: A Life,* is built on mountains of research and writing by others, of which I am a deeply grateful beneficiary. Most of the researchers and interpreters have been associated with the impressive Works of Jonathan Edwards project at Yale University. I am especially grateful to my friends and former students Kenneth Minkema and Harry S. Stout for their personal help as well as their recent leadership in that project, but there are too many other major contributors to mention here. More complete acknowledgments as well as documentation of their impressive contributions can be found in the larger volume. Edwards's own works, including his previously unpublished sermons, notebooks, and the like, can be found online under the Works of Jonathan Edwards. Some quotations new to this book from Benjamin Franklin are from well-known sources. In chapter four I was newly guided regarding Whitefield and Franklin by Frank Lambert, *"Pedlar in Divinity": George Whitefield and the Transatlantic Revivals* (Princeton University Press, 1994), pp. 97-99, 110-30, and regarding the awakenings generally by Thomas S. Kidd, *The Great Awakening: The Roots of Evangelical Christianity in Colonial America* (Yale University Press, 2007). For the account of Edwards and the Suffield awakening in chapter five I have used new material from Douglas L. Winiarski, "Jonathan

Edwards, Enthusiast? Radical Revivalism and the Great Awakening in the Connecticut Valley," *Church History* 74:4 (December 2005), pp. 683-739.

I am very appreciative to Thomas S. Kidd and Sarah Miglio for reading a draft of this manuscript and making many useful suggestions for improvements. I am also grateful to David Bratt for his very helpful work in editing. My thanks are due also to Andrew Baxter White for his expert work on the index. As always, my greatest debt is to Lucie. She is well named.

CHAPTER ONE

Edwards, Franklin, and Their Times

—⁓⁓⁓—

At the beginning of October 1723 two remarkable young New Englanders, unknown to each other, dearly hoped to settle in the city of New York. Had they both succeeded, the story of early America would include dramatic accounts of close interactions and conflicts between the two most renowned colonial-born figures of the era. New York City, a town of less than ten thousand, might not have been big enough for the both of them. As it turned out, the New York hopes of both Benjamin Franklin and Jonathan Edwards were quickly dashed, and the two probably never met.

Two Young Men in British America

Benjamin Franklin's New York quest is part of a familiar tale. Not quite eighteen, he broke his printer's apprenticeship with his brother James and secretly embarked on a sloop bound for New York. After delays due to contrary winds, he eventually arrived at the formerly Dutch seaport only to find that the sole printer in town, William Bradford, needed no help. Bradford nonetheless suggested that the young man try his luck in Philadelphia, where Bradford's son was a printer and looking for help. The rest is legendary.

During the same weeks that Franklin was visiting New York, Jonathan Edwards, having spent the summer at his parents' home in East Windsor, Connecticut, was holding out a last hope to return to the city where he had spent the previous fall and winter. Just turning twenty on October 5, 1723, he had already served as an interim pastor in that cosmopolitan town not far to the south. The young man's months in New York were among the sweetest in his memory, and he had formed some deep personal attachments. He was hoping he might be called back there as the regular pastor of the city's Presbyterian church. But the existence of such a position depended on first healing a schism between the English and Scottish factions of Presbyterians in the city. In October a delegation sent by Edwards's alma mater, Yale College, reported that the schism could not be healed. There was no opening for Edwards. He would have to wait four more years before finding a venue suited to his high personal and spiritual ambitions.

Franklin and Edwards, although about as different in both temperament and commitments as they could be, also had a lot in common. They were both products of the Calvinist culture of New England, and they both came of age in the eighteenth century, when it was an open question as to how the ways of the old Puritan experiment could survive in the self-confident modern world of the British Empire and the Enlightenment. Franklin and Edwards responded to this juxtaposition of eighteenth-century British modernity and New England's earlier Puritan heritage in almost opposite ways. They represented two sides of the same coin in the emerging American culture during the era before the American Revolution. Each grew to be one of the most influential figures in the British colonial culture of the mid-1700s. Each is better understood if we keep in mind that he lived in the same relatively small colonial world as the other and dealt with many of the same issues.

In the case of Jonathan Edwards it is especially helpful to be reminded that his life paralleled that of the *pre-revolutionary* Franklin.

Edwards died at age fifty-four in 1758, at a time when no one envisioned the coming break with Great Britain. Franklin lived until 1790, so we remember him as a revolutionary. If he also had died in his mid-fifties (and he did almost die while crossing the Atlantic in 1757), we would have a very different picture of him. He would still be remembered as a great wit, as British America's most famous scientist and inventor, especially for his electrical experiments, as an ingeniously practical civic leader, and as prophet of inter-colonial unity. Yet he would also have been a figure always loyal to the British Crown (he, in fact, did not give up that loyalty until the eve of the revolution), and as a slave owner (until 1781), considerably less progressive in some of his social views than the Franklin we usually remember.

Edwards and Franklin, though opposite in temperament, were both sons of pious New England Calvinist families at a time when their heritage faced a severe crisis. Each was precocious and, growing up in an era when print dominated the media, each read everything he could get his hands on. Each as an extraordinarily curious boy delved into the mysteries and rigors of the theological volumes in his father's library. In their teens each admired the witty writings of England's *Spectator,* edited by Addison and Steele. Each soon realized that the Calvinist theology that dominated New England's intellectual life was sadly out of date according to fashionable British standards. Edwards and Franklin each spent a lifetime dealing with the clash of these two worlds. Each worked vigorously to use what he saw as essential in his New England heritage to meet the challenges of a rapidly changing modern age.

If we think of the Puritans as one of America's first immigrant communities, then the opposing reactions of Edwards and Franklin to the dramatic transitions of their era becomes the prototype of a classic American story. A community founded on faith as much as on ethnicity divides within itself over how to adapt to the ways of a new era. In later times we would say these conflicts were about

"Americanization," although in the era of our protagonists it was more a debate about becoming British, or "Anglicization" as it is sometimes called. Franklin embraced the progressive culture of his day with a vengeance, so much so that he forsook family, religion, and region to seek his own fortune. Edwards faced many of the same challenges but held onto the old faith. He did so not as a reactionary but was, like Franklin, an innovator. His experience of intensely held Calvinism in the era of the cool reason of the Enlightenment resulted in remarkable creativity.

Young Edwards may have read the younger Franklin. In May 1722 (the year before they both wished to settle in New York) Ben's creation, Silence Dogood, made her fourth appearance in James Franklin's *New England Courant.* In all likelihood this issue of the controversial paper soon found its way to New Haven, Connecticut, where Edwards was a student at Yale, since the subject of the Widow Dogood's ridicule was Harvard College, already Yale's archrival. Following the example of John Bunyan's popular Protestant classic, *Pilgrim's Progress,* the widow reported that she had fallen asleep and had awakened in a land in which "all places resounded with the fame of the Temple of Learning." Approaching this famed institution, she found its gate guarded by "two sturdy porters named Riches and Poverty, and the latter obstinately refused to give entrance to any who had not gain'd the favour of the former." Inside the Temple, the ignorance and idleness of the students was covered up by their dabbling in Latin, Greek, and Hebrew. Widow Dogood, curious to find why so many flocked to study in the "Temple of Theology," soon discovered Pecunia (money) lurking behind a curtain. The students, "following the contrivances of Plagius," copied into their own works the words of the popular anti-Calvinist Anglican preacher, John Tillotson, known for his eloquence.

Franklin's satire would have amused Edwards, since Yale students stood ready to believe the frequent rumors of doctrinal laxity at Harvard. Edwards's father was a conservative Connecticut clergyman and had been a firm supporter of his colony's alternative to Harvard ever since the younger school's founding in 1701. Jonathan himself had no illusions about New England college students. Even though the majority of his fellow Yale students were, as he was, studying theology, he found most of them to be a rowdy bunch. He could easily imagine that things were even worse at Harvard.

Clever satirist that he was, Franklin often made Widow Dogood speak as though she were a country conservative shocked at what she found in fashionable Boston. In one early contribution she noted that "among the many reigning vices of the town" to be deplored was the sin of pride, "a vice most hateful to God and man" — especially, she lamented, the growing evidence of "pride of apparel." This vice was most pronounced among her own sex, as evidenced by the ridiculous fashion of "hoop petticoats," which she said were so massive that they might be stacked at the local fort to scare off invaders. In an earlier day, plain dress had served as an identifying feature of Puritan New England. The early settlers deplored ostentatious displays of wealth. Now times were changing, as many of the third- or fourth-generation heirs to the Puritan heritage, even if still subscribing to the formal tenets of the old faith, were dropping its austere forms and adopting English fashions, no matter how extravagant or bizarre.

Much of what the clergyman's widow said deploring "pride of apparel," modern styles, and displays of wealth sounded just like sermons that either young Jonathan or young Ben might have heard. New England's Congregational clergy were the most revered men in the provinces. They were the best educated and had long held a near-monopoly on public speaking, preaching at least two sermons a week. Their churches were "established" as state institutions supported by taxes. They were usually full, due to either law or custom. Clergy also spoke often in weekday lectures and on public occasions, such as election days. They all professed Calvinist orthodoxy, but they differed in temperament between those who were more

5

forward-looking moderates, more lenient on matters such as styles of dress, and stricter conservatives. In outlying areas such as the Edwardses' Connecticut, or in western Massachusetts where Jonathan's famous grandfather, Solomon Stoddard, presided, conservatives held firm control. Boston was more cosmopolitan and also more divided. Aging Increase Mather and his anything-but-silent son Cotton Mather, whose *Essays to Do Good* inspired Franklin's pseudonym, led the Boston conservative pastors who lamented that Puritanism's glory years were becoming dim memories.

The rise of newspapers in Boston of the 1700s had the potential to challenge the clergy's dominance in public communication, a potential that became a reality when James Franklin established the *New England Courant* in 1721. Patterning his paper on the witty London *Spectator,* he immediately used his paper to attack Cotton Mather. The occasion later proved to be notoriously ill-chosen, although at the time the merits of the case were far from clear. Mather was championing inoculations as a way to reduce risk during a devastating smallpox epidemic, and Franklin sharply assailed him for what seemed to him a dangerous experiment. Mather, despite his rigid theological conservatism and nostalgia for the old days, knew more about contemporary science than anyone else in the colony, an expertise that had gained him membership in England's prestigious Royal Society. The first source of Mather's knowledge about inoculations was from Mather's slave, Onesimus, who assured him they were a common practice in Africa. Mather, a person of insatiable curiosity, not only confirmed Onesimus's testimony from other slaves, but soon read of the success of such practices in the Ottoman Empire as reported in the Proceedings of the Royal Society. Many Bostonians, including most of the physicians, opposed Mather's inoculation program. Someone even firebombed Mather's house. James Franklin, capitalizing on the controversy, helped lead this chorus of opposition probably largely because Mather represented the conservative establishment. In June of 1722, after the smallpox crisis had passed, the establishment struck back. The Massachusetts General Court, apparently looking for an excuse to silence the insubordinate *Courant,* threw James into jail for a month for some seemingly mild sarcasm about the government.

Ben Franklin found himself temporarily in charge of publishing the *Courant,* and simultaneously Silence Dogood shed her guise of a conservative. In the first issue after James's imprisonment, the widow's entire letter was a long excerpt from the *London Journal* on freedom of speech. "This sacred privilege is so essential to free governments," she quoted, "that security of property, and freedom of speech always go together; and in those wretched countries where a man cannot call his tongue his own, he can scarce call any thing else his own." This quotation reminds us that young Franklin would eventually grow to be a revolutionary, but as he and his readers were well aware, the seeds of revolution had been planted by their Puritan forebears themselves. Silence Dogood's quotation goes on to cite the memory of "the Court of King Charles the First," in which "his wicked ministry procured a proclamation, to forbid the people to talk of parliaments, which those traitors had laid aside."

Franklin thus invoked the most momentous political event in Puritan history. In 1649 English Puritans and the parliament under Oliver Cromwell emerged as some of the first modern revolutionaries when they executed King Charles I as a traitor. In New England, the revolutionary heritage persisted. In 1689 New Englanders celebrated the "Glorious Revolution," when the Protestant prince, William of Orange, replaced the Catholic James II. Out of that second revolution had grown what in England became known as the "commonwealth tradition" (Cromwell had overseen a Puritan "commonwealth" before English kings were restored), which championed principles of liberty over against tyranny. By mentioning Charles I, the widow was pointing to the irony of the Boston Court's suppression of political criticism: the heirs to Puritanism were much less open to dissent when they themselves held power than when they lacked it.

Silence Dogood followed this salvo with a letter two weeks later deploring hypocrisy. As in earlier pieces, she had chosen a topic that was a staple of New England sermons. Now, however, she turned the familiar theme into an attack on the close alliance between the clergy and colonial officials, who might use pious language for their own purposes. *"A little religion,"* she pointed out in an aphorism that still rings true, *"like a little honesty, goes a great way in courts"* — that is, in politics. This was especially true "if the country . . . is noted for the purity of religion."

Jonathan Edwards would have agreed with Franklin's views on hypocrisy in principle, even though as a son and grandson of ministers who was entering the ministry himself he was a beneficiary of New England's political-religious establishment. In later life, even though his political instincts were conservative, he was ready to criticize magistrates who hid behind a mask of piety.

Yet if Jonathan happened to read the *Courant* of July 22, 1722, he may have become suspicious about the widow's own piety. Franklin began her letter with a version of a classic New England sermonic question: "whether a commonwealth suffers more by hypocritical pretenders to religion or by the openly profane." Schoolboys like Edwards debated such issues. Yet in his zeal to expose the ruin that hypocrites in public positions might bring to an entire country, Franklin minimized the dangers of open irreverence by private individuals. "A notoriously profane person in a private capacity," Silence opined, "[only] ruins himself, and perhaps forwards the destruction of a few of his equals."

Here, slipped in unobtrusively, was a capsule of Franklin's life philosophy that we know so well from later writings. To Franklin it seemed self-evident that moral principles should be determined only by weighing the consequences of actions. For instance, in his *Autobiography,* when he recounts his early attempts at reaching "moral perfection" by following a list of virtues (such as Frugality, Industry, Sincerity, and the like), he redefines the virtue of "Chastity" in a way that allows for wide personal freedom: "Rarely use venery [gratification of sexual desire] but for health or offspring, never to dullness, weakness, or injury of your or another's peace or reputation." Franklin thus articulated what became one of the most pervasive American traditions, one that countless people would use, as he did, to free themselves from religiously-based moral strictures of their various communities of origin.

Edwards, on the other hand, exemplifies a very different but equally American story. Edwards's story, like that of countless since, was one of meeting the challenge of remaining loyal to a nurturing traditionalist community, even when the attractions of cosmopolitan modern life, like a centrifugal force, threaten to pull the community apart and destroy its distinctiveness. As in most such communities, the counteracting centripetal force that held it together was not only loyalty to family, friends, and the community itself, as inestimably important as those were, but also a loyalty to a transcendent religious ideal. Faith and trust in God made loyalty to the community not just a matter of personal choice, but rather a matter of high principle seen as linked to nothing less than one's eternal destiny.

An Immigrant Community's Religious Heritage

By the very nature of the case, there is no fully typical story of American experience, so as we might expect, the community into which Edwards grew up had some singular traits. The Puritans who settled New England were the first and the largest, and therefore by far the most influential, of the ethno-religious communities in the British colonies. Further, the unusual circumstance of having been usually a persecuted minority in their home country of England but an overwhelming majority in their American settlements created some long-term tensions that we need to consider in more detail.

While the tens of thousands of Puritans who left for America in the 1630s were part of an oppressed religious group in England, they had long aspired to rule. At the time, in the midst of well over a century of warfare and struggle between Protestants and Catholics that followed the Reformation, most people took for granted that a nation should have only one religion. If one religion was the only true one, most people reasoned, then it made no sense that the state should tolerate false substitutes. Such tolerance, the reasoning continued, would result in the state failing to protect its citizens from the greatest danger of all, that of being betrayed in the matter of their eternal life. Protestant success accordingly depended upon winning the sympathies of a nation's rulers. The Puritans were "Reformed," or part of the Calvinist movement (named for the sixteenth-century Genevan reformer John Calvin) that was the first international movement for revolution and national reform of modern times.

In this Reformation battle for the loyalties of monarchs and hence their nations, England itself was a peculiar case. In 1534, less than two decades after the Reformation began, King Henry VIII decided to change churches in order to change wives. England thus became Protestant, but its reasons for doing so were so weak that it was particularly liable to revert to Catholicism. In fact it did just that from 1553-1558 under Queen Mary, one of Henry's daughters who remained Catholic despite her father's reform efforts. Under another daughter, Queen Elizabeth, a Protestant, who reigned from 1558-1603, a compromise set the Church of England on an unusual course. Its theology would be Protestant, but its forms would resemble Catholicism. Bishops would govern the church, and its worship would include much of the imagery, pomp, and rituals characteristic of its Catholic heritage.

Puritanism was simply the name given to a more radical group of Calvinist Protestants who wished to carry the Reformation further by "purifying" the Church of England. They wanted to eliminate any Catholic-like forms, images, and practices and set up a "pure" church in which the Bible alone would be the guide for faith, life, and worship. Hoping to gain these reforms, Puritans evangelized within the Church of England to win converts to their cause. Ultimately, though, control of the state church would depend on governmental support.

Since Queen Elizabeth I (the "virgin queen" for whom the colony of Virginia was named) had no children, the English monarchy in 1603 passed to the House of Stuart, which had little sympathy for the Puritan party within the Church of England. By 1630, even though Puritans had secured some support in the British Parliament, their prospects looked so bleak in England that tens of thousands of them risked the long, dangerous trip to settle in America. In the 1640s, however, the situation in England changed dramatically when a civil war broke out. Eventually, the party of Puritans and the Parliament triumphed, leading in 1649 to the unforgettable execution of Charles I. With the king gone, Oliver Cromwell, a Puritan army general, ruled England as a commonwealth.

Following the death of Cromwell in 1658, the anti-Puritan House of Stuart was restored in 1660, and during the next decades the government persecuted and repressed Puritans in England. In 1685 James II, a Roman Catholic, came to the throne. Protestants of the Church of England responded in 1688 and reasserted their dominance, in what they called the "Glorious Revolution," by driving James into exile and declaring that the throne would always be Protestant (as it still is by law). The Church of England remained the established church, while the heirs to the Puritans (Congregationalists, Presbyterians, and Baptists), were now officially tolerated as "dissenters." Because they were not of the Church of England (or Anglicans), dissenters were excluded from significant political positions and even from attending the major universities, Oxford and Cambridge.

Meanwhile the distant province of New England developed somewhat differently, as immigrant communities always do. The original Puritans who settled Massachusetts and Connecticut had ruled pretty much as they wanted. Following the usual practice of the era, they established their own churches and excluded all others. During the revolutionary times in the 1640s and 1650s they had close ties with English Puritans, but after the restoration of the Stuarts they were left isolated. In 1684, late in the era of Stuart rule, they lost their virtual independence. Eventually Massachusetts received a new charter that gave them a royal governor and required them to tolerate other Protestants. Connecticut retained its original charter but, like Massachusetts, had to adopt English ways of at least tolerating other Protestant groups. Still, both colonies saw their tax-supported Congregational churches retain establishment status and virtual monopolies in most towns.

The dual heritage of the Puritan immigrants — in England oppressed and hence champions of their rights, while in their colonies promoters of their own religious monopolies — left some tensions that were still unresolved even in the early 1700s, when Jonathan Edwards was coming of age. When others held political and ecclesiastical power New Englanders were quick to talk about their God-given "rights." When they themselves ruled, however, most New Englanders believed that subordinates should willingly submit to God-ordained authorities.

In a ministerial family such as the Edwardses', the most troubling element of this dual heritage in the 1700s had to do with the nature of the church. Was the church, as the "puritan" label of its forebears suggested, supposed to be a pure institution made up of believers only, or should it be more inclusive to reflect its establishment status? Their forefathers had built plain unadorned meeting-houses to signal that what made a church was not its buildings or adornments, but the presence of the Holy Spirit among the body of true believers gathered for worship. They therefore examined prospective members closely to make sure they had just the right signs that their hearts had been transformed by the Holy Spirit. By the middle decades of the 1700s, however, standards were changing in many congregations. The most visible manifestations of that change can still be seen today in New England church architecture. Gradually eighteenth-century New Englanders replaced their plain meetinghouses with the lovely spired church buildings that grace the New England countryside. These "Georgian" style buildings reflected a more general spread of British tastes among the heirs of the original plain-styled immigrants. The corresponding change, which would lead to some of the greatest drama and pain in the life of the Edwards family, was that standards for church membership were changing. In some places, Congregational churches were beginning to move in the direction of becoming more like parish churches of the old world, in which everyone would be baptized into the church and standards for adult membership were not terribly strict.

Jonathan was born into the conflicts these unresolved issues would create. His father, the Rev. Timothy Edwards, was a strict proponent of the old ways. Timothy demanded that prospective communicant members of the church (people who could partake of "communion" or the sacrament of the Lord's Supper) be able to give a precise account of their journey from rebellious sinner to regenerate ("born again") convert. He did not expect them to recount a moment of sudden conversion, but rather they should tell of a step-by-step progress resulting in a certifiably transformed life. New Englanders like Timothy Edwards did not expect perfection among their parishioners. Rather they looked for something more like that found in John Bunyan's bestseller, *Pilgrim's Progress* (published 1678-1684), an allegorical account of a man's journey to the celestial city in which, though his heart has been changed by God's grace, he still often loses his way. For Timothy Edwards, telling the difference between imperfect saints who recognized the need for total dependence on God and self-deluded hypocrites who professed religion but followed their own desires was a science that demanded his expertise.

Whereas Benjamin Franklin by his early teens rejected this whole Calvinistic enterprise and ever after celebrated trust in himself, for Jonathan Edwards the overarching question in life would be whether he and others were truly regenerate. From his early days Jonathan could not escape the haunting syllogism that if the creator of reality was a personal being who had revealed his perfect love in Jesus Christ, then by far the most important issue in life was one's relationship to God. That was what regeneration was about. He knew that by nature he was in his heart of hearts a rebel against God who rejected God's love. His only hope was that God would transform his rebellious heart so that he could know and respond to the overwhelming love of God as revealed in Jesus Christ's death on the cross for sinners. Yet since remnants of self-centered sin remained even in the hearts of saints, it was often excruciatingly difficult to be sure whether one truly loved God or was a self-deluded hypocrite. Edwards's coming of age, until his early twenties, was dominated by that struggle. While Franklin would celebrate his rebellion against old authorities, Edwards would find through his struggles with them deeper meanings that shaped his sense of mission not only to his native New England but also to the trans-Atlantic world of the Enlightenment.

CHAPTER TWO

Wrestling with God

By the time Jonathan Edwards was a boy of ten or twelve, perhaps the most striking element of his household in the village of East Windsor, Connecticut, was the sheer number of girls it contained. Jonathan eventually had ten sisters, four older and six younger. His mother, Esther, daughter of the Reverend Solomon Stoddard, the most influential man in western New England, was also a formidable presence. So while there was no doubting the authority of his father, Jonathan grew up surrounded by women. As the only boy, he was a center of attention. From early years his parents groomed him for college and the ministry, and his older sisters often oversaw his lessons. Throughout his life Jonathan especially admired female piety, which he saw first in his mother and sisters.

Timothy Edwards ran a tight ship. Even if his talented wife Esther was practically in charge of household matters, we know from letters that Timothy wrote while briefly serving as a chaplain in the army that no domestic detail was too small to escape his oversight ("Let care be taken that the . . . barn door ben't left open to the cattle"). He ran his church the same way, meticulously gauging the spiritual condition of any candidate to become a full communicant member and always expecting everyone to defer to proper authority. Timothy dearly loved his children, but it was the love of a micromanager. He had the highest expectations for his only son. The attentive father was an excellent teacher of Latin and Greek, the languages necessary to enter college. Jonathan was a born student, and his remarkable aptitudes must have gratified his father immensely.

Piety

Jonathan was intellectually precocious enough to meet the demands of a perfectionist father, but in another way he could never quite measure up. Nothing mattered nearly as much as the state of one's soul. Eternity was at stake. The concern was urgent — sudden death might strike at any time. Every child remembered playmates that had died. Who would be prepared? Parents reminded children from an early age that even the greatest worldly learning, acclaim, or success would be worth nothing if one's heart were fixed on something other than God. Those who served self and success alone would be condemned to suffer miserably in hell for eternity, as the Bible taught.

The catch was that in Calvinist New England no amount of effort could earn heaven. Salvation was by God's grace alone. For strict Protestants like Calvinists, this was the most basic principle that separated them from Catholics. It also separated them from what they saw as more lax Protestants (often loosely called "Arminians"), who they believed had reintroduced the idea that everyone had the power to do some good works that would help contribute to their salvation. Calvinists, or the strictly "Reformed," wanted to give God all the credit. Jesus had said, "Ye must be born again" (John 3:7), and being born, as Calvinists pointed out, was not something one did for oneself. No amount of learning, no amount of striving, could create a heart that truly loved God.

At the same time, Puritans in New England did not just sit back and wait for God's grace to strike, living it up in the meantime. Indulging one's own passions could harden one's heart against God.

And godly habits, even if they earned no merits, could help prepare one to be open to God's grace. Such exercises could also clear the way of some of the obstacles, such as love of vices that blinded many from seeking God. So pious New Englanders like the Edwardses, despite their emphasis on grace, insisted on good works as much as anyone. They lived under strict discipline of law and practices of piety. Every child knew the Ten Commandments and was taught to observe them to the letter, as much as was humanly possible. Every day and every meal began and ended with family or personal prayers and devotions.

Such routines could be tedious and even have a negative effect. Benjamin Franklin once again provides a good illustration. Always practically minded, the boy found the long and repetitious family prayers boring. So to save time he suggested to his father that he might bless the whole cask of salted fish at once, rather than praying over it every time it was served. Ben's father, a wise and pious tradesman, had hoped and prayed that his brilliant youngest son would enter the ministry and had even sent him for a time to the Latin School, the first step toward Harvard. After a year he withdrew him, pleading the financial strains of a large family. The boy's skeptical turn of mind, if not a cause of the change in course, soon confirmed that he would never make it among the orthodox clergy.

Young Jonathan was in many ways a pious child. For a few months at age nine he was even excessively pious, building a secret hideout in the woods for prayer. Yet he could also, like any boy, get into trouble and be impatient with the endless religious rituals. He found lengthy church services tedious. Still, he seemed to be under the spell of his impressive father, and he wished more than anything to please his parents with evidences of true religion. When Jonathan was twelve, Timothy Edwards oversaw a stirring revival in his church, one of several during his ministry, and Jonathan wrote excitedly to one of his sisters reporting on the results. Even so, he himself, despite his best efforts, did not show the heartfelt love of God that was a sign of true conversion.

Intellect

Later that year, Jonathan entered college, just as he was turning thirteen. He was younger than the average student, but such an early start was not so unusual, since the only requirement for college entry was skill in Greek and Latin. When Jonathan began college the "Connecticut Collegiate School" was operating in three locations under three tutors. Jonathan went to Wethersfield, not too far from home, where the tutor was his talented young cousin, Elisha Williams. By Edwards's fourth year, the college had been consolidated in New Haven and renamed Yale. Jonathan completed his B.A. in New Haven and then stayed on for over a year to work on an M.A. under the formidable new rector, Timothy Cutler.

As a brilliant and inquisitive teenager Jonathan wrestled with the largest intellectual issues of his day, and these intense inquiries shaped his outlook for his entire life. When he got to New Haven the newly acquired Yale library gave him access to the books that were fomenting an intellectual revolution shaking the Western world at its foundations. During the previous half-century the scientific revolution, best symbolized by Isaac Newton (1642-1727), had changed the way many educated people were looking at things. Among many leading thinkers, scientific principles, based on reason and discovery of natural laws, were becoming the model for truth in all areas. In philosophy the most influential figure was John Locke (1632-1704), who wrote both about natural laws that governed how we know things and about natural laws on which to base government. Newton and Locke were both Englishmen, and we must remember that the New England colonists still thought of themselves as British. Inquiring young men, such as Jonathan in New Haven or Ben Franklin in Boston, who had been weaned on the theology of dogmatic Protestantism now had to cope with disconcertingly new ways of thinking.

Jonathan encountered these new ideas in a more controlled atmosphere, but his recognition of their implications seems to have created a more painful struggle than it did for the teenaged Ben, who was always ready to throw off any yoke that restrained him. Jonathan, shaped as he was by an intense and passionately pious family, was temperamentally disposed to hold on to the heritage of those he loved, but that made the intellectual challenge even more intense. He later recalled that during his teenage years, when he first encountered the writings of John Locke, he studied them with the enthusiasm of "the most greedy miser in gathering handfuls of silver and gold from some new discovered treasure."

Even before reading the modern authors, Jonathan had been wrestling with the standard objections to the paradoxes of his Calvinist heritage. Particularly, he later wrote, "from my childhood up, my mind had been wont to be full of objections against the doctrine of God's sovereignty, in choosing whom he would to eternal life, and rejecting whom he pleased, leaving them eternally to perish, and be everlastingly tormented in hell. It used to appear like a horrible doctrine to me." These were not new issues — they repeatedly appeared in the history of the Christian church. If God was all-powerful and good, how could he permit evil? Why would he allow some of his creatures to be punished eternally? Especially if, as Calvinists taught, salvation was based wholly on God's grace and not at all on one's own merits, how could it be that a just and good God chose from eternity to redeem some people and allow others to be damned? Calvinists and their predecessors in the tradition of St. Augustine (354-430) argued that all these doctrines were plainly taught in the New Testament, but many others throughout church history had raised the same objection that Jonathan had as a boy. Making the challenge more intense, Jonathan grew up at a time when it was fashionable for many of the best educated to question and revise dogmatic traditions in the light of the new learning that celebrated humans' natural abilities to know truth and to live morally. In England, where memories of Puritans' brief rule only two generations earlier were still fresh, most sophisticated thinkers took for granted the rejection of Calvinism.

For Jonathan these issues were much more than abstract theory. Everything in life depended on them. Most importantly, whatever his doubts and the condition of his heart, he was convinced that his eternal destiny was at issue. The stakes were incredibly high. Even many of the liberal Christians of the era still believed in some sort of heaven and hell. Edwards always wondered how it was that people who affirmed such beliefs could take them lightly. If one weighed eternal happiness or suffering against any earthly love or concern, there was no comparison. One should be willing to give up anything if it threatened one's *eternal* state.

As a teenager Jonathan agonized all the more deeply over the state of his soul because it had deep emotional implications in relation to his family. His parents, Timothy and Esther, insisted that his eternal destiny was more important than any other concern. Some of his sisters seemed more genuinely pious than he, and they too longed deeply for his salvation and kept it in their prayers. Jesus had said that "there is no man that hath left house, or parents, or brethren, or wife, or children for the kingdom of God's sake who shall not receive manifold more in this present time, and in the world to come" (Luke 18:29-30). For Jonathan such statements had paradoxical implications: finding true love for Jesus would be a way of fulfilling his parents' fondest hopes.

Conversion

The overwhelming struggle came to a head during his senior year at Yale, when Jonathan was overtaken by a violent illness, pleurisy or chest disorder, and believed he was going to die. It was, he later wrote, as though God "shook me over the pit of hell." He did what any sixteen-year-old might do when facing death: he promised to mend his ways. Soon after his recovery, though, he found that "I fell again into my old ways of sin." But now it seemed that God would not let him rest. He had "great and violent inward struggles: till after many conflicts with wicked inclinations, and repeated resolutions, and bonds that I laid myself under by a kind of vow to God, I was brought wholly to break off all my wicked ways, and all ways of known outward sin; and to apply myself to seek my salvation."

This heroic effort at self-improvement, we know from his diary of a couple years later, had serious ups and downs. It did help clear some obstacles, but it did not bring the joy of a change of heart. Nonetheless, as he much later described it using a Calvinist framework, God began working in ways that were not the direct result of Jonathan's efforts.

First, quite remarkably, his longstanding objections to God's sovereignty suddenly disappeared. He remembered the occasion vividly, but for a long time afterward did not see in it any special work of God's Spirit. Rather, it seemed like an intellectual breakthrough that resolved a host of interrelated intellectual issues in which he had been deeply absorbed. Like many of the great thinkers in this era immediately after the Newtonian revolution in natural science, Edwards was attempting to understand how everything in the universe fit together. For him, it all fell into place when he realized that the central theme of his own heritage — the sovereignty of God — could be the solution to finding the grand scheme of things. God's sovereignty had been a problem for Edwards because he had been *underestimating* its awesome implications.

Edwards now saw that the universe was essentially personal, an emanation of the love and beauty of God, so that everything, even inanimate matter, was a personal communication from God. So in contrast to many contemporaries, such as Franklin, who saw Newton's laws of motion as providing the model for understanding an essentially impersonal universe, Edwards started with a personal and sovereign God who expressed himself even in the ever-changing relationships of every atom to each other. This dramatic insight would be the key to every other aspect of his thought. Like a mathematician who had discovered an elegant solution to an immense problem, Edwards was captivated by the beauty of the insight. He now found the doctrine of God's sovereignty "a delightful conviction."

Corresponding to the intellectual breakthrough was the beginning of dramatic experiences that were more recognizably spiritual. In them he was overwhelmed by "a new sense, quite different from anything I ever experienced before." This new sense was a "sort of inward, sweet delight in God and divine things." Such experiences, which recurred throughout his life, clearly were related to his intellectual breakthrough. Once he understood the grandeur, goodness, and glory of God in large enough terms, he began to have life-changing emotional encounters with the beauty of God. These compelling experiences of beauty might come, as the first one did, simply from meditating on a Scripture verse, 1 Timothy 1:17, that spoke of God's greatness and glory. Or they might well up while he contemplated "the loveliness and beauty of Jesus Christ." Or he might be overwhelmed while walking alone in the fields considering the works of creation, the sun, the moon, trees, flowers, or even thunder. He saw each of these as part of God's language. They were "types," or figures built into creation that pointed to God's attributes, and ultimately to the love of Christ.

During the first year and a half after such experiences began, Jonathan was completing his senior year at Yale and then continuing there in his M.A. work. In August 1722, after his first M.A. year (residency was not required), he left New Haven to serve as a supply pastor of a small Presbyterian church made up mostly of New Englanders in New York City. Still only eighteen when he arrived, he fell in love with the small but thriving seaport on the tip of Manhattan Island. His love was closely related to the family with which he lived. Madam Susanna Smith was a widow from England, and Jonathan became closely attached both to her and to her son John, his own age. As in all his closest relationships, Jonathan loved John as a spiritual soul mate. The two young men would wander the wilds of Manhattan, taking in the beauties of the Hudson River, and (as Jonathan later recalled) speaking often of God's coming kingdom and of the glories to be expected on earth in the last days.

Despite his dramatic experiences and insights of this era that changed his life and set the basis for his mature outlook, Jonathan's spiritual progress was also a struggle. True to his Puritan heritage and his father's teachings, his conversion, as he experienced it, was no sudden transformation in which he could name the day and the hour, as in later evangelicalism. Even so, Jonathan worried that the process did not seem to follow the exact steps that his forebears had identified. Despite an intensity of experiences that would have satisfied most people, Jonathan continued in "great and violent inward struggles" to purge his faults so as to prove to himself that his transformation was genuine.

While he was in New York, Jonathan wrote an elaborate set of strict resolutions and began keeping a diary that tracked his day-to-day efforts to follow them. Once again we can see both a parallel and a contrast to Benjamin Franklin, who similarly set for himself a list of "virtues" so that he could acquire good habits. Franklin's virtues were designed for self-fulfillment; Edwards's were designed to subordinate his own will to God's will. As he put it in Resolution 43: "Resolved, never henceforward, till I die, to act as if I were anyway my own, but entirely and altogether God's." His specific resolutions included trying to give up pride and vanity and trying to obtain strict discipline in eating and drinking, not speaking ill of others, and cultivating patience and serenity in place of anxiety. Even while Jonathan resolved to renounce his own self-centered desires in favor of God's glory at all times, he did not see such giving up of natural desires as contrary to his ultimate self-interest. Rather, he was trying to live in the perspective of eternity. No sacrifice of time, energy, or desire in this world even began to compare to the endless joys of those who were united with God forever.

It was one thing to make such a thorough and impressive list of resolutions; it was another to keep them. This we know from his diary, in which he reported his efforts fairly regularly for the next year or two. Although he noted the spiritual highs that he later recalled, his diary also records many days of lows, "decays," and lengthy times of inability to focus on spiritual things. Clearly at times he was distracted and disconcerted by his inability to wholly control his lusts, although he was very guarded in references to such things. His emotional swings during a time of particular spiritual intensity suggest a lifelong pattern. Edwards later described himself as sometimes prone to "melancholy," something like what we would call a mild form of depression. At times in later life he felt so weak that he was almost unable to face other people socially. He managed these difficulties through the strictest disciplines: keeping up his routines of prayers and devotional study of Scripture and following his resolutions against wasting any time, Edwards literally worked his way through his bouts with melancholy.

Although preaching every week in New York City must have added to the pressures of his life, Jonathan's time there came to an end far more quickly than he would have liked. When he had to leave in April, he "had a most bitter parting with Madam Smith and her son." As he sailed away he kept the city in sight as long as he could and continued to long for it "with a kind of melancholy mixed with sweetness."

He spent a long and sometimes difficult summer in 1723 back at home with his parents, wondering what he should do next, and hoping for a call back to New York. In the meantime he had to prepare an address for the Yale commencement in September, when he would receive his M.A. That would be a sort of debut before the assembled clergy of Connecticut, and he was anxious both that he excel and that it be seen as evidence of his thorough orthodoxy. In his spare time he worked on polishing up an essay he had written on his intriguing observations of flying spiders, hoping to get it published by the Royal Society, England's great scientific body headed by Isaac Newton. Like many of the great thinkers of this era that were so influenced by Newton's work, Edwards always had an interest in the new natural science. In his youth, that was one of his favorite pastimes. In his notebooks he kept observations on the implications of Newton's theories of light and on how the new physics might fit with God's sovereignty. His observations of spiders that could gracefully float in the air were his only effort in empirical science to survive. While Edwards's work was worthy, most of his otherwise original observations had, unknown to him, been anticipated by the English naturalist Martin Lister, so the young colonial's piece was not published.

Jonathan was ambitious to serve God in some dramatic way. Even though he was only nineteen, he had already been laying plans to write some great treatises on theological and philosophical subjects. He had begun keeping expandable notebooks of "Miscellanies," which he would continue throughout his life, for drafting his thoughts on such topics. He also began other notebooks for thoughts on interpreting Scripture and prophecy. In one of his earliest notebooks he wrote down some rules for writing. These including revealing observations that "the world will expect more modesty because of my circumstances — in America, young etc." and that people are jealous of "upstarts." Clearly planning to be such an upstart, he also mused on how he might get published in London.

His most immediate concern during the summer of 1723 was the momentous one of where to launch his career. Returning to New York was his first choice, but that possibility was fading. He even at some point contemplated a sojourn in London (which would have occasioned another parallel to young Franklin), but Jonathan's father apparently feared the corruption of the Old World city. A pastorate was open in North Haven, near New Haven and Yale, and Jonathan also had hopes for that. His father, in the meantime, had been pushing him toward accepting a call to pastor a small country church of Bolton, Connecticut, about fifteen miles from East Windsor. That was not an attractive choice for an aspiring young man who longed to participate in the cosmopolitan thought of the day. Finally, by November, when nothing else had come through, Jonathan reluctantly signed on to be pastor at Bolton. The New York dream was gone, and he settled into a crossroads parish.

CHAPTER THREE

Transitions and Challenges

—❦—

The crossroads hamlet of Bolton, Connecticut, was a far cry from New York City. Jonathan's winter among the sometimes-quarrelsome Yankee farmers, after the excitement of his seaport stay, was one of discontent. Yet, in another occasion for his oscillating temperament, the spring brought unusual joy. His only later mention of Bolton was that he recalled "having one special season of uncommon sweetness: particularly once at Bolton, in a journey from Boston, walking out alone in the fields." We know from his notebooks in which he reflected on "Images of Divine Things" that his spiritual sensibilities were often renewed by enthralling experiences of the beauties of nature as types or images of God's love in Christ. "When we are delighted with flowery meadows and gentle breezes of wind," he wrote, "we may consider that we only see the emanations of the sweet benevolence of Jesus Christ; when we behold the fragrant rose and lily, we see his love and purity." Green trees and fields and the singing of birds were "emanations of his infinite joy and benignity." "That beauteous light with which the world is filled in a clear day is a lively shadow of his spotless holiness and happiness and delight in communicating himself."

New Haven

This trip from Boston must have been in May, when New England ministers often gathered for Election Day there, and Jonathan's renewal of spiritual joy may have been sparked by the knowledge he would soon be leaving Bolton. He had received an appointment to be a tutor back at Yale College. Returning to his alma mater with its impressive library collection, and to a place where he would be socially visible again, must have been an attractive prospect for the bookish and ambitious twenty-year-old.

Jonathan had another reason to rejoice at the prospect of moving to New Haven. Already in the previous fall, he had written a tender prose poem to a young girl, Sarah Pierpont, whose spiritual beauties he admired. "They say there is a young lady in [New Haven]," he wrote, "who is beloved of that almighty Being, who made and rules the world, and that there are certain seasons in which this great Being, in some way or other invisible, comes to her and fills her mind with exceeding sweet delight, and that she hardly cares for anything, except to meditate on him." Her meditations were "after a while to be . . . caught up into heaven" where she would be "ravished with his love, favor, and delight." This communication with God and contemplation of eternity gave her "a wonderful sweetness, calmness and universal benevolence of mind" so that she was not tempted by worldly treasures or fearful of earthly pain.

Jonathan apparently inscribed this idealized spiritual portrait of Sarah in the flyleaf of a book he presented to her when she was still only thirteen and he nineteen. Sarah was the daughter of the late Rev. James Pierpont, and the two ministerial families may have been close. The Pierpont home was just across the New Haven Green from Yale College. Jonathan was also a friend of Sarah's older brother, James Pierpont, who was sometimes a tutor at Yale. So Jonathan had many opportunities to observe the spirituality of the young girl whom he idealized and admired.

Whatever euphoria Jonathan may have experienced in moving back to New Haven was, true to form, short-lived. Colonial colleges had summer terms and commencements in September, so the young tutor was immediately thrust into the role not only of teaching and hearing recitations every day but also of keeping order. Students, who ranged in age from thirteen to their early twenties, tended to be unruly, and Jonathan never had the best rapport with those who were coarse, irreverent, or defied authority. His responsibilities were especially difficult at Yale, since the college lacked an older resident rector to keep things in order. Two years earlier, to the great consternation of much of New England, Yale's learned rector, the Rev. Timothy Cutler, had announced that he was joining the Anglican Church. Most New England Congregationalists were still close enough to their Puritan roots to see Anglicanism as an enemy, so there was no doubt that Cutler must resign. To make matters worse, the Yale trustees had not been able to find a suitable replacement. Though local clergy helped oversee the school, Jonathan and his fellow tutors were pretty much on their own.

In September 1724 Jonathan crashed spiritually, suddenly hitting the worst and most prolonged religious crisis of his life. Commencement season was when college boys most often let loose — the previous year trustees had assessed students for broken glass in the dormitories and set up fines for "any public disturbance by hollooing, singing or ringing of the bell unseasonably, firing guns, or otherwise." Near this time Jonathan recorded that "Crosses of the nature of that, which I met with this week, thrust me below all comforts in religion." Whatever happened, he was spiritually unprepared for it, and three weeks later he noted that something connected with the commencement had "been the occasion of my sinking so exceedingly." Not until three years later did he feel that he had recovered from this misery.

We do not know what this crisis was about, or whether the troubles around commencement season were the *cause* of his troubles or only the *"occasion"* for it. Much later he referred to it as "some temporal concerns, that exceedingly took up my thoughts, greatly to the wounding of my soul." That would suggest some larger persistent issue, but there is no way to be sure.

There is a possibility — although this is sheer speculation — that the crisis had something to do with his courtship of young Sarah Pierpont. We have only a few solid facts. Jonathan had his eye on Sarah already when he wrote his spiritual tribute, apparently in 1723, the year before he moved back to New Haven. By May or June of 1725 he and Sarah were engaged to be married two years from then. Sarah was only fifteen at the time she was betrothed. While seventeen would be far younger than the New England average for women to get married, it was not outside of the bounds of propriety. Nor, apparently, was an early engagement when the two families were agreed. Nonetheless, some sort of courtship or at least friendship presumably began before the engagement and could well have gone back to the fall of 1724, when Sarah was still only fourteen. However spiritual this early relationship may have been, the transition toward engagement may have encountered a rocky start — or at least raised eyebrows.

Once the engagement was approved in the spring of 1725, the relationship could still have been a distraction from spiritual things. We have to remember the height of his spiritual standards. In Jonathan's view, every temporal matter should point to a higher meaning. During his years of engagement he wrote a number of remarkable meditations on such themes in his extensive "Miscellanies" notebooks, indicating that at least sometimes he was catching sight of the heavenly realities for which he sought.

One of these gives us a hint about his early relationship with Sarah. "The best, most beautiful" way, he wrote, "of expressing a sweet concord of mind to each other, is by music." For Jonathan a social relationship was "in the highest degree happy" when people were "expressing their love, their joys, and the inward concord and harmony of spiritual beauty of their souls by sweetly singing to each other." Singing together was an anticipation of the perfect communion of souls in heaven.

Whatever the nature of their growing relationship, Jonathan often reminded himself that earthly loves should always point to Christ's redemptive love. In another entry from the same time he remarks, doubtless with Sarah in mind, that "beautiful airs of look and gesture" make us immediately think that "the mind that resides within is beautiful." Edwards, as we have seen, considered the world to be filled with signs that pointed to higher realities, so this observation that a beautiful look or gesture signaled a beautiful inward spirit immediately reminded him of a still higher truth: the beauties of the universe are signs of the beauty or the excellencies of Christ. "How greatly are we inclined to the other sex!" he wrote late in the spring of 1725. "Nor doth an exalted and fervent love to God hinder this, but only refines and purifies it." Here the spiritual lesson was that "Christ has a human nature" and experienced love for other humans. For Christ this love was "to the church, which is his spouse." The church as "the bride of Christ" was one of Jonathan's favorite biblical images. Among his favorite books of the Bible was the Song of Songs, also known as the Song of Solomon, which is in the form of a poetic celebration of the earthly beauties of lovers and was conventionally interpreted in Edwards's day as an image or type of the love of Christ for his church.

In one entry, written around January 1726, Jonathan reflects on the contrast between earthly and heavenly love. "How soon do earthly lovers come to an end of their discoveries of each other's beauty, how soon do they see all that is to be seen," he writes. After they have been "united as near as 'tis possible, and have communion as intimate as possible," soon "no new ways can be invented, given or received" for expressing their love. Heavenly love, by contrast (and also in contrast to a common image of heaven as a sort of fixed euphoria) will be a love for Christ forever growing, changing,

31

and becoming more spiritually intimate. This account of the limits of earthly love, written more than a year before he was married, was common enough in literature for Jonathan to have known about it only secondhand. Nonetheless, the exceedingly high standards of spirituality, asceticism, and chastity that he maintained for himself and others might make us wonder about the role of sexual attraction in distracting him from realizing the high spiritual expectations he demanded of himself. His spiritual standards were like those of a monk, but, true to Protestant principles, he was pursuing his spiritual ideal not in a separated community, but in the everyday world and through an engagement to be married.

Northampton

Jonathan's life took another monumental turn during this same period. His grandfather, the Reverend Solomon Stoddard, was aging. The most renowned man in all of western New England, Stoddard had been pastor of the church in the significant town of Northampton, Massachusetts, since 1672. At eighty-three years of age he was looking for an assistant and successor, and he was rumored to be looking especially among a number of his ministerial grandsons. Jonathan's candidacy for this position may have been delayed in the fall of 1725, when he fell desperately ill and nearly died. But in the fall of 1726 he won the much-sought-after position and moved to Northampton, where he was ordained as assistant pastor.

Jonathan's place in Northampton was very much a family affair. In the eighteenth-century British world of which New England was a part, most things were run through hierarchical networks of personal dependencies. Servants (including African slaves in the Americas) depended on their masters, women and children were dependents on male heads of families, apprentices were subject to their masters, the poor depended on the generosity of the rich, and aristocratic families administered justice and dominated politics. Even the aristocrats were themselves ultimately dependent on the patronage of the royal governor, who in turn was dependent on the king. In New England, where there were very few persons of nobility, a natural aristocracy had arisen among powerful networks of the families of leading clergymen and magistrates. The clan associated with Solomon Stoddard was a prime example. Stoddard's sons and grandsons were intermarried with other influential families, most notably the Williams family of whom we shall hear more, who with their allies ran most of western New England through a series of personal networks.

When Jonathan moved to Northampton, still as a single man in the fall of 1726, both his grandfather and grandmother Esther Stoddard were still living, and he probably moved in with them in a substantial house overlooking the town. Also living in the family home was the Stoddards' second son, Colonel John Stoddard, aged forty-four in 1726 (he finally married and started his own family in 1731), the most powerful magistrate in the region. John Stoddard's patronage for his young nephew was almost as important as that of Solomon Stoddard. John was a sort of baron for the town. He was the most important judge in the region, the most important military leader, a significant landowner, the town's most frequent elected representative to the Massachusetts General Court (legislature), often a member of the Governor's Council, and the leading layman in the governing councils of the church.

Jonathan's marriage to young Sarah Pierpont on July 28, 1727, was a decorous affair suited to the New England aristocracy to which both belonged. The only surviving hint about the details is a bill that Jonathan saved, dated January 26, 1727, from Boston, for items including buckles, white gloves, and a lute string. These must have been for the wedding, which means the occasion included the playing of instrumental music. That small detail is noteworthy, since New England Congregationalists, true to their Puritan heritage, did not use musical instruments in church services. Nevertheless, also faithful to that heritage, marriage was a civil ceremony — emphasizing their departure from the Roman Catholic view that marriage was one of the sacraments — so instrumental music was appropriate. The Edwardses' home would soon become known as a place of music and singing, and Sarah herself may have played an instrument, such as the lute, as women of the time often did.

During his years as a tutor in the midst of his spiritual doldrums, Jonathan had almost abandoned his diary. Marriage, however, seems to have precipitated a change that he felt worth recording. About two months after the wedding, he wrote that it was "just about three years, that I have been for the most part in a low, sunk estate and condition, miserably senseless to what used to be, about spiritual things." Now, just about the same time of year as the disastrous commencement season of 1724, he rejoiced that "I began to be somewhat as I used to be." Perhaps the spiritual companionship with Sarah was the key to his recovery. Perhaps it was that the married state transformed his sexual desire from being a spiritually demoralizing distraction to a gift of God to celebrate. Perhaps his spiritual depression had been related to the loneliness and insecurities of being a tutor among unappreciative students. Or possibly some of his doubts about Reformed theology persisted, even as he was sketching out impressive defenses of it against its enlightened critics. We do not know. In any case, their marriage led to a renewal of the spiritual sense that was so central to his life and thought.

Squire John Stoddard made sure that the town treated the heir apparent and his young wife suitably to their status. Jonathan and Sarah received funds sufficient to purchase a "Mansion house, barn and home lot of three acres" in the town, ten more acres for a pasture, and forty acres further from town that could be used for income in addition to a solid salary. After little more than a year the house (large for then, though not so by our standards) began to fill further when their first child, Sarah Jr., was born. During the next twenty-two years, ten more children (seven girls and three boys) would follow almost at regular two-year intervals. Remarkably, in this time of high mortality at all ages, all would survive childhood.

Meanwhile, Jonathan's responsibilities increased dramatically with the death of Solomon Stoddard in February 1729. The patriarch, who lived into his eighty-sixth year, remained a formidable presence until the end. Although his eyesight was failing, his mind was sound, and he was still able to preach effectively without notes. Stoddard had come to Northampton nearly sixty years earlier, so there was almost no one in the town who knew of any other leadership than his. It is difficult for us today to imagine what influence a clergyman might wield in an inland New England town, and even by those standards Stoddard had unusual power, enhanced by the family network of magistrates and clergy that made him the leading spokesman for the whole region. He was old enough to remember the days of Oliver Cromwell's Puritan commonwealth in England of the 1650s, and he retained the Puritan ideal of a holy society in which church and civil magistrates worked hand in hand to foster true worship and righteous behavior. In Northampton, Stoddard was revered and feared, sometimes loved, sometimes resented. His supremacy was unchallenged. Jonathan later wrote that the people of Northampton regarded him "almost as a sort of deity." When the great man finally died, his grandson faced the awesome task — at which many capable people have failed — of stepping into the shoes of a formidable predecessor.

Momentously for Jonathan, Stoddard had not been simply a conservative champion of the past; rather, he had left a legacy of controversial innovation. Stoddard modified some conventional Puritan practices — but only, as he saw it, in order to preserve the essence of the Puritan heritage. The issue that Stoddard addressed, and which Jonathan would have to wrestle with throughout his years in Northampton, grew out of a central dilemma in American Puritanism. As we saw in the first chapter, Puritans thought the true church should be made up only of (carefully scrutinized) regenerate believers. But as reformers who were, technically speaking, still connected to the Church of England, Puritans were also heirs to the ideal of Christendom in which "the church" included every generically Christian person in a parish. Early Puritans in New England, despite their separatist or "sectarian" pure-church ideals, retained some important elements of this European heritage of an "established" church: they required everyone in a town to attend church services, and they supported the church with public taxes.

This tension particularly manifested itself, in Northampton and elsewhere, when the time came for children to be baptized. In England before the American settlements, Puritans had been critical of the Church of England's practice of baptizing all "Christian" children born in the parish and routinely confirming them once they became young adults as full church members who could partake in the sacraments. At the same time, they longed for the broader churchly influence offered by that approach.

To make a long story short, Solomon Stoddard, who entered the ministry some forty years after the first settlements, had devised a way to cut through this tension between ideals that had long troubled New England church life. In Northampton he broadened the standards for full church membership to all adults who professed the doctrines of the church, submitted to its discipline, and promised to attempt to live morally. Such broader standards meant that most if not all upright citizens of the community were likely to become full members of the church. So the citizenry of the church and the citizenry of the town became more or less co-extensive. Stoddard also accepted a broader standard for baptism, one that was already being adopted in many New England towns by the time of his entry into the ministry in the 1670s. Called "the half-way covenant," this policy provided that even if adults, who had been baptized as children, did not become communicant members, their children could be baptized. In other words, God's covenant, as Puritans referred to

God's promises and of which baptism was a sign, extended to the grandchildren of believers as well as to their children. By combining the half-way covenant with the broader standards for communicant membership, Stoddard had reestablished something very much like the old parish system of Christendom.

Stoddard's innovations in Northampton, which were adopted in many other western Massachusetts churches as well, were controversial and set off a colony-wide debate that lasted for decades. Stoddard's principal critic was Increase Mather (1639-1723), Boston's most influential conservative pastor, rivaled only in his later years by his son and close ally, Cotton Mather. For the Stoddards, the Mathers, and the Edwardses, this lengthy dispute reflected the powerful family dynamics mentioned earlier — with a twist. In Northampton Stoddard had succeeded Increase Mather's brother, the Rev. Eleazar Mather, who had died while in his early thirties. Solomon Stoddard succeeded Eleazar Mather in more than one respect when he married Mather's widow, Esther Warham Mather Stoddard (ca. 1640-1736). That meant that Jonathan Edwards's mother, a daughter of Solomon Stoddard, had half-siblings from the Mather family. To complicate the family dimension of the debate, Jonathan's father, Timothy Edwards, was close to the Mathers and took their side in the controversy.

Although the Mathers were the conservatives in this debate, that did not make Solomon Stoddard a liberal. Rather, he was another kind of conservative, one who was willing to innovate in order to preserve what he believed to be the essence of Puritan tradition. In this respect, he was one of the first in a long line of American Protestant conservative innovators, one that included evangelists who readily adapted their messages to demands of new audiences (and their styles to new technologies). In Stoddard's case, he was adapting the Puritan heritage to the needs of a frontier town on the western edge of the colonial settlements. In practical terms, by keeping the memberships of the town and church more or less co-extensive, he increased his authority over the entire town, making most of its citizenry subject to the discipline of the church. Traditional Puritan that he was, Stoddard firmly believed that Christian communities in modern times stood in the same relationship to God as did Old Testament Israel. If the community kept God's laws, it would be blessed. If it blatantly defied God's laws, it would be punished by God's judgments. Hence, the more authority the pastor had in overseeing the morals of the town, the better off everyone would be.

In addition to this authoritarian dimension of Stoddard's outlook, there was another aspect that had much more to do with the Puritans' emphasis on grace, rather than their conspicuous concern for law. Stoddard believed as much as any early Puritan that the goal of the church was, through God's grace, to bring people to wholehearted commitment to God — that is, to conversion. He just did not believe that it was necessary to be *sure* people were in that state before they were allowed full membership and to partake in communion. The sacrament of the Lord's Supper, he believed, might be a "converting ordinance," or the occasion for a decisive spiritual transformation, as he thought it had been in his own experience. Too strict a standard for communicant church membership might keep some people who were truly seeking God from participating in one of the principal "means of grace."

For the practical-minded Stoddard, fostering conversions was more important than discovering a perfect church order, and in that attitude he blazed the way for the most influential practice in American religious history: he was the first American to make periodic revivals a centerpiece of his ministry. Every decade or so Stoddard's Northampton congregation experienced a remarkable "awakening" in which many people were moved to see the depth of their spiritual need, often leading to conversion and a new outlook guided by the Holy Spirit. Although Stoddard was the most successful preacher in the region in promoting such awakenings, he was not alone in the enterprise. Some of these revivals were regional, breaking out in a number of towns simultaneously. They had a direct impact on Jonathan's immediate family as he was growing up: his father, who rejected the half-way covenant but embraced revival, presided over two such awakenings in East Windsor. Whatever others thought about Stoddard's theory, they could not quarrel with his results. In 1714 the aging Increase Mather wrote a preface to Solomon Stoddard's latest book on evangelism, *A Guide to Christ,* signaling a truce between the "brothers" over the unresolved questions of church membership.

Nevertheless, the disagreements surrounding the half-way covenant that had divided the family and the region remained unresolved, and eventually would have momentous consequences for Jonathan Edwards. When he came to Northampton he was probably more inclined to agree with the stricter views of his father rather than with his grandfather's more open policy regarding communicant membership, but for the time being, an agreement to disagree seems to have prevailed. The opportunity to join and then succeed his grandfather in the largest church in western Massachusetts was too good for Jonathan to give up, and he seems to have made a good-faith decision to live with a policy about which he had some scruples. As for both his father and his grandfather, the larger issue in ministry for Jonathan was to help awaken people to their need to trust in Christ alone.

CHAPTER FOUR

Awakening

New England's occasional awakenings and other efforts to revive piety were part of an international "pietist" movement. Early eighteenth-century New England was not only a far-flung province of Great Britain, but also an outpost in a larger European Protestant culture. Puritanism itself had been the English version of a vigorous international Calvinist or "Reformed" movement that had been working to win all of Christendom to the Protestant cause. By the second half of the 1600s, though Protestant-Catholic conflicts continued, it was clear that Europe would remain divided. After the end of the devastating Thirty Years' War in 1648, Protestantism found itself on the defensive, or at least in a weakened state. In some areas Catholic interests were resurgent and Protestants suffered persecutions. In other areas either Calvinist or Lutheran Protestantism was established as the state church. By the latter part of the century, much of this state-sponsored Protestantism was suffering from the sort of hardening of the spiritual arteries that is common to causes that have lost their youthful vigor. Being Protestant was sometimes little more than a cultural loyalty into which people were born, and its old ways were protected by codes of confessional orthodoxy. Pietists knew that the combination could be deadly.

Pietism and Revival

Pietism was a loosely organized movement of common responses throughout the Protestant world to such losses of vitality. While usually remaining doctrinally orthodox, pietists emphasized the "religion of the heart." Individual commitment was their primary way of authenticating the faith. That emphasis reflected a much broader tendency in European culture to begin to place a premium on individual "self" as a source for establishing authenticity. Trends as diverse as that set by the philosopher Rene Descartes (1593-1650) with the famous starting point, "I think, therefore I am," to a new dependence of rulers on the popular support of their subjects reflected the wider developments of emerging individualism. Such new emphases on the self, the individual, or the people are usually associated with the dawning of the modern era, and pietism was a religious expression of such an early modern impulse to value individual experience.

The big difference from more secular emphases on the self, however, was that when pietists emphasized individual experience as the proof of faith, theirs was most essentially the experience of dependence, rather than of independence or self-sufficiency. Pietism centered on self-renouncing acts of devotion to God in spiritual disciplines and evidences of true spirituality in self-sacrificing deeds of charity and missions to help others. One did not possess the natural ability to do such good, but rather one needed to be transformed by the Holy Spirit working within. The often-contagious dynamic of the movement grew out of this new emphasis on the work of the Holy Spirit, resulting in visibly transformed lives marked by good works.

One of the most famous of the German pietist leaders, August Hermann Francke (1663-1727), for instance, proposed a "Great Project for a Universal Improvement in all Social Orders" and was widely known for founding an orphanage and educational institutions designed ultimately to improve the social order. Francke's influence also illustrates how pietism developed as an international move-

41

ment. He published his country's first newspaper and maintained an immense correspondence with some five thousand persons, including a core network of four hundred regular correspondents.

Early Puritanism had been one of the forerunners of pietism, and the early eighteenth-century heirs to Puritanism in New England had much in common with the newer international movement. One of Francke's regular correspondents was Boston's Cotton Mather, Increase Mather's remarkable son and associate. Cotton published indefatigably on every subject imaginable, and he helped keep New Englanders in touch with the European developments. Mather, like Francke, was constantly proposing projects for reforming everything, as in his famous *Essays to Do Good.* Benjamin Franklin, growing up in Mather's Boston, is often seen as a secular heir to such reforming zeal. That, by the way, helps explain why later, during the height of international pietism's influence in the colonies, Franklin became close friends with the renowned visiting British evangelist George Whitefield.

Northampton Awakened

Solomon Stoddard's Northampton, which Jonathan Edwards inherited in 1729, had long been one of the far western outposts of international pietism. Like Francke in Germany or Cotton Mather in Boston, Stoddard had aspired to transform everything in society according to the dictates of the faith. Pietists often emphasized that people of faith needed vital local communities as their bases of operation. Northampton, with perhaps a thousand citizens, was already such a community — at least some of the time. Stoddard had been able to hold sway over the town as pretty much his own bailiwick. He himself had long been a spokesman to the colonial government for the interests of western Massachusetts, and during his last decades had solidified his family's political and judicial influence especially as his son John emerged as the village squire, leading magistrate, military leader, and pillar of the church. When it came to moral oversight in Northampton, the bounds between church and civil authority were hard to distinguish.

Such a tightly ordered society, while exhibiting some potential to be a model pietist community, was also bound to breed discontent. Religious fervor is never easily passed on from generation to generation. Jonathan later wrote that the people of Northampton had never "been the most happy in natural temper." Rather they had, "ever since I can remember, been famed for a high-spirited people, and close, and of a difficult, turbulent temper." The volatility of their perennial discontent had its opposite counterpart in this two-sided town in the periodic revivals — almost as though once in a while things would get so bad that a collective sense of a need to turn back to God would sweep over the town.

In between revivals, subcultures that provided alternatives to the church culture thrived. The town's taverns, of which there were already three when Jonathan arrived, were favorite social centers. Puritans had allowed alcoholic beverages if not used to excess, and taverns, which did not require much more than a room and a table to set up, were a natural part of an English village. Farmers and other townsmen gathered there to relax and conduct business. In times of political discontent, which was frequent in Northampton, taverns were likely the places to hear about it.

As far as Jonathan was concerned, the most formidable challenge to church piety was a well-developed youth culture, which intersected with the tavern culture. One practical issue contributing to the strength of this youth culture was that young people were often postponing marriage: the *average* age of marriage had risen to twenty-nine years old for men and twenty-five for women. The primary reason for postponing marriage was a shortage of land. New England towns were organized on a communal basis. Almost everyone lived in the town itself on garden-sized plots of land and also owned other detached tracts of farmland distributed around the outskirts. Northampton families typically had five to nine children, so the population was rapidly increasing. About a generation before Edwards arrived, the supply of open land had run out. So prospective young couples now were finding it difficult to establish themselves independently of their parents.

As a result, a large group of restless young people in their twenties dominated Northampton's youth culture. Jonathan later observed that when he arrived in Northampton, the young people were disturbingly out of control. In church services, for instance, they showed disrespect for the once-mighty Solomon Stoddard, by now enfeebled and nearly blind.

Nonetheless, even during Stoddard's latter days, Jonathan and the old patriarch had seen a glimmer of hope for revival. The occasion was a rare earthquake that shook New England. On Sunday evening, October 29, 1727, a sharp quake brought down chimneys and a few walls. More importantly it and a number of aftershocks stoked fears that God was warning of greater judgments to come. Well-educated New Englanders by now understood that earthquakes had natural causes, but most everyone, whether well-educated or not, *also* believed that God sent warnings and judgments through natural calamities. In many New England towns, the jolts set off awakenings. Northampton experienced a small revival, the last under Stoddard, who estimated twenty converts. Some weeks later Jonathan, preaching on a special day of fasting and communal repentance, reiterated the prevailing view of the quake's meaning, especially its timing. New England Sabbaths began and ended at sunset, and on Sunday evenings it was customary for the young people of the town, after a long day of religious services, to congregate and stay late into the night for "frolics" filled with "mirth and jollity." The earthquake, Edwards admonished, was not only a judgment on New England's sins generally but likely was for "more especially the sin that is committed on a sabbath-day night."

The youth of the town were apparently not long impressed by such warnings, and soon their subculture was again thriving. Edwards recorded that after Solomon Stoddard's death in early 1729, their disrespect for authority grew even stronger for a time. Eventually, however, Jonathan's passionate intensity and clarity of vision began to have an impact. After two or three years, the young people seemed to soften, to listen more attentively in church, and to moderate their "frolicking."

During the winter of 1733-34 the young pastor, seeming to have gained the ear of his unmarried parishioners, pushed to further these reforms. He preached against "company keeping" between the sexes, especially on holidays and on Sabbath-day evenings. "Company keeping" often led to sexual transgressions. All over New England, the number of premarital pregnancies was rising — in fact, it had become hardly unusual for the first child of a young couple to be born less than seven months after their marriage. Edwards, drawing on the long-standing patriarchal principles of the society, at first emphasized that "company keeping" should be a matter of family discipline. He called on the men who were heads of households in various districts of the town to exercise their authority over their unmarried grown children. Remarkably, the plan seemed to work: parents reported that at district meetings where they discussed the issues, the young people agreed that they needed to exercise more restraint.

A dramatic event soon turned this favorable atmosphere into a full-fledged awakening. In June 1734 one of the most admired young men in the town was stricken with a sudden illness and died two days later. Edwards seized the occasion. Addressing a congregation in a state of shock, he preached a poignant sermon on Psalm 90:5-6: "In the morning they are like grass which groweth up. In the morning it flourisheth and groweth up. In the evening it is cut down and withereth." Depicting an image of strikingly beautiful flowers of the field that are mowed over and ruined by the end of the day, Edwards reminded the weeping congregation of the fleeting beauty of youth. Having himself been near death on a couple of occasions, he spoke with deep passion on how foolish it was to center one's life on short-lived pleasures. Who knew whether he or she would be the one laid out in the coffin the next week? When friends stood by such a young person's deathbed, "how shocking it will be to think that this is the person that . . . was so lewd a companion," and spent "leisure hours so much in frolicking." How much wiser it would be to trust in Christ, whose beauty far outshone the highest earthly glory, and in whom one's joy would be for all eternity.

Edwards often reiterated the positive side of this message as well as its negative warnings. When a young married woman was taken ill just a few weeks after the death of the young man, and then she seemed dramatically changed and testified to others of her love to Christ before she died, Edwards preached on the joys of knowing that a departed loved one was with the Lord. Speaking to special gatherings of concerned young people, he emphasized that Christ's love bound them together now and for eternity as no earthly love could.

This glorious vision of higher spiritual love in this world and the next spoke to the anxieties of the young and began to dramatically transform their culture. By the fall of 1734, instead of frolicking on Sunday nights and Thursday evenings after weekday "lecture" sermons, the young began meeting in homes throughout the town for "social religion," or times for singing, Bible study, and prayer. Soon adults all over the town were doing the same.

As the awakening was gathering strength, Edwards published perhaps his greatest sermon, one that encapsulated some of the most characteristic themes in his theology. Originally preached in 1734, "A Divine and Supernatural Light" presented a concise summary of Edwards's years of theological reflection and his answer to life's most essential question: what did it mean to have one's heart changed in a true conversion experience? As in all his theology, Edwards started with the premise that God was the primary actor in any relationship. God was always communicating his love and beauty. Scripture often compared this revelation of God's goodness to light. The beauteous light of God's love was always shining around us, but not everyone truly saw it. Some might even know about it in theory, but this did not mean they had a true experience of what it was like.

To have that experience one needed "eyes to see" or "ears to hear," as Scripture put it, or a sort of sixth sense. That transforming spiritual sense was itself a gift of the Holy Spirit. The difference between a mere knowledge *about* God's love in Christ and a true spiritual *experience* of the beauty of that love was like the difference between knowing that honey was sweet and actually tasting the sweetness of honey. Sinful people were so preoccupied with their own pleasures that they never glimpsed God's true love. Once their eyes were opened to see the beautiful and wondrous love of the perfect Christ's sacrifice for undeserving sinners such as themselves, they would be so drawn to that beauty that their hearts would be changed. Their most fundamental disposition would be to love God and whatever God loved.

Such preaching, centering on God's love in Christ and the intense love to God it should bring in return, had its effect. Toward the end of December 1734 the awakening took another dramatic upturn and moved to a level of intensity that Edwards thought was unprecedented even in his grandfather's ministry. A young woman known as "one of the greatest company keepers in the town" came to Edwards with what he judged to be a sincere profession of conversion. The news of this was "almost like a flash of lightening" among other young people. The young woman was now testifying to her most notorious company-keeping friends. Soon "awakened" young people were gathering in lines at Edwards's study door seeking spiritual counsel.

By the spring the whole town seemed caught up in an amazing

fervor of awakening. According to Edwards, people talked of almost nothing but spiritual things. They dwelt on other topics only so long as it was necessary to conduct their daily work, and they even sometimes neglected their work so that they could spend more time in spiritual activities. Even sickness almost disappeared for a time, Edwards reported. Normally parishioners would hand him "prayer bills," mentioning illnesses for which they requested prayers in the church service. During the height of the awakening, there was not a single such request "for many Sabbaths together." People of all ages, including some children and many people over forty, were converted. "Several negroes" were among those appearing to "have been truly born again" and received into church membership. Although Edwards acknowledged that only God knew whether hearts were truly and permanently changed, he judged that in a town of perhaps a thousand inhabitants, as many as three hundred seemed to have been added to the ranks of the spiritually transformed.

Astonished by the phenomena that surrounded him, he made a momentous decision — he decided to write a precise account of the revival. Following the model of the scientific reports of the day, in which careful observers sent detailed accounts of natural phenomena for dissemination among other scientists, Edwards wrote a "faithful narrative" of "this surprising work of God" to be sent to fellow clergy. In so doing he would greatly amplify and perpetuate the potential impact of the awakening. Edwards addressed his lengthy account to the leading clergyman in Boston, the Rev. Benjamin Colman, who had already indicated interest in the amazing stories of the awakening that had spread even to some of the most influential clergy in England.

On the first Sunday of June 1735 the awakening took a shocking turn — one that forced Edwards to break open the seal of his just-completed narrative and add a grim postscript. On the morning of that Sabbath one of the town's leading citizens, Joseph Hawley, slit his throat and died in an act of despair. Hawley, who owned a local store, was married to one of Solomon Stoddard's younger daughters, a sister of Edwards's mother. He was given to deep melancholy, a malady that ran in his family, and the coroner "judged him delirious" at the time of his death.

Edwards was devastated by "Uncle Hawley's" suicide. He explained it, characteristically, at two levels: the psychological and the spiritual. Hawley was given to deep melancholy, a malady that ran in his family. The coroner "judged him delirious" at the time of his death. Edwards had counseled with Hawley during the awakening and recognized his uncle's despair at his inability to find sufficient signs of grace. Nonetheless, Edwards also believed that God often used despair to bring sinners to true recognition of their need to depend on God alone. So even though he found Hawley beyond guidance by mere reason, Edwards continued to preach forcefully that those who did not receive grace were doomed to eternal punishment. Above all, when Hawley took his own life, Edwards interpreted it as an episode in a cosmic spiritual struggle. "Satan seemed to be more let loose" and "raged in a dreadful manner" in order to destroy the awakening. As might be expected when there was a mighty work of God, Satan (whom Edwards, true to the Christian heritage, regarded as a real personage) would furiously strike back.

Uncle Hawley's suicide dampened the awakening fires. In fact, as the news of Hawley's awful death spread throughout the region where many revivals were in progress, so did something of a suicide craze. According to Edwards, "multitudes," including many pious people who suffered from no melancholy, were seized with a sudden temptation, as though someone was saying to them, "Cut your own throat, now is good opportunity: *now,* NOW." Most resisted, but a few succumbed. The craze helped snuff out the spiritual contagion of the awakenings.

To Edwards and other proponents of the awakenings, these "most awful providences," in which God in his mysterious ways permitted Satan to act, actually confirmed the spiritual nature of the events. Edwards remained optimistic about the long run. Satan's days were numbered; God's kingdom would come, and his people would be delivered from the power of the Evil One. In the meantime, the grand spiritual struggle centered in Christ's death and resurrection would continue throughout human history. Even as Satan desperately flailed to counter the effects of Christ's redemptive triumph, worldwide awakenings would mark the advance of the Holy Spirit in these latter days.

Even as Edwards grew discouraged by the waning of the revival in Northampton and the Connecticut Valley, he could look abroad to see some unexpected effects his account was having in helping to spark the very sort of international awakening for which he prayed. Boston's Benjamin Colman was deeply impressed by Edwards's account of the awakening, the grim postscript about Joseph Hawley's death notwithstanding. Colman sent a copy of the letter to a couple of correspondents in London, Isaac Watts and John Guyse. Isaac Watts was a clergyman famed in the English-speaking world both as a great hymn writer and as a polymath who wrote books on a wide range of subjects. Guyse was a pastor of one of the leading dissenting (non-Anglican) churches in England's capital city. Thrilled by the news from New England, Watts and Guyse wrote to Colman to ask if they could get a fuller account of Edwards's amazing story that they could publish.

Edwards promptly wrote a lengthy account and sent it to Colman, who immediately published a shortened version as an appendage to some sermons he was seeing through the press for Edwards's uncle, the Rev. William Williams of Hatfield. Williams, married to yet another Stoddard daughter, was the successor to Solomon Stoddard as the leading clergyman in Hampshire County, as the western half of Massachusetts was called. Since Hatfield was only a few miles from Northampton and it had also enjoyed an awakening, Colman assumed that it was natural to bind the works of uncle and nephew together. Edwards was a bit embarrassed, however, that this was done without his notable uncle's permission. It is certainly possible that his uncle was not entirely happy with an account of the regional awakening that put Northampton so much at the center.

Colman sent the full Edwards account to Watts and Guyse, who had it published with some editing (not always for the better — they changed Hampshire County to New Hampshire on the title page). This work went through several editions, including an American one that Edwards had restored to the original. It was prefaced by a brief attestation, signed by William Williams and five other local pastors, assuring that "the account Mr. Edwards has given in his narrative of our several towns or parishes is true; and that much more of the like nature might have been added with respect to some of them."

By the time that American edition finally appeared in 1738, the Connecticut River Valley awakening was history, but in Great Britain and even on the continent it was still inspiring news. *A Faithful Narrative of the Surprising Work of God* was republished in 1737 and 1738 in Edinburgh, and in a German edition in 1738.

In Great Britain the moment was right for the publication to make an impact that no one could have anticipated. Beginning in late 1736, George Whitefield, a young Anglican evangelist just out of Oxford, began an itinerant (traveling) ministry in London and elsewhere that drew considerable attention. At Oxford Whitefield had become close friends with John and Charles Wesley, who had founded a "holy club" and were known as "Methodists" for their rigorous quests for a deeper piety. In 1738 Whitefield interrupted his fledgling preaching career to follow John Wesley as a missionary to the new colony of Georgia. By the time Whitefield arrived, Wesley had left, but Whitefield developed what became a lasting interest in the New World before he too returned to England in 1738. In the meantime what would prove to be the modern evangelical movement had suddenly begun to blossom. That same spring, John Wesley, who had been ardently seeking true religion for years, had a dramatic spiritual experience in which he felt his "heart strangely warmed" only a few days after his brother Charles's own conversion experience. The Wesley brothers' ministry soon flourished and would eventually become the huge Methodist movement. Whitefield, who before long would go his own way, aided the new movement by the innovation of preaching outdoors. The crowds this young preacher drew were immense, often to tens of thousands — some of the largest gatherings, except for armies, ever seen.

Edwards's *Narrative* was among the inspirations for the Wesleys, Whitefield, and their associates. John Wesley later edited a version of it for his Methodist followers. In Scotland the *Narrative* had a similar impact in Presbyterian circles; it was often cited as a model that helped spark a "great awakening" in that rugged country in the early 1740s.

Whitefield

The sensation caused by Edwards's account among Watts, Guyse, the Wesleys, Whitefield, and the Scots demonstrated the power of the printed word to advance their cause. At the same time as Whitefield took preaching to the fields outside the confines of the church doors, so the power of the press could rapidly spread the infectious news of remarkable revivals. As printing became more efficient, news quickly became national and international. Today we take for granted having media that enable people everywhere to follow the same event; it is hard to imagine a day when almost everything was essentially local. The utilization of the press by the new evangelical movement was an early expression of the kind of widely shared popular culture we have now. Much the same thing soon spread to popular political movements — the American Revolution, for instance. But evangelical religion was one of the first instances of this now-familiar trait of the modern world, a media-based spread of a popular outlook and style.

George Whitefield carried his ministry, and this modern way of promoting it, back to the New World. Newspaper reports of the immense crowds to which he preached in England early in 1739 made him a sensation even before he arrived in Philadelphia later that same year. Preaching outdoors, even in the chill of November, he drew crowds estimated at six to ten thousand — astonishing numbers for a city with a population of only thirteen thousand. Whitefield fascinated Benjamin Franklin, publisher of the city's leading newspaper. During one sermon Franklin walked backward as far as he could still hear Whitefield clearly, which was about five hundred feet beyond the crowd. He estimated that in an open field up to forty-five thousand people would have been able to hear. This convinced the skeptical Franklin that reports from England that Whitefield had preached to twenty-five thousand at a time could be true.

Benjamin Franklin, despite his liberal views on religion, had many reasons to like Whitefield, and the two soon became good friends. When Whitefield came back to Philadelphia on his several trips to the colonies their friendship deepened — as did their business connection, not incidentally to Franklin. Whitefield was already a boon for publishing, especially through his *Journals,* in which he recounted his revival activities. They were already selling widely in the Atlantic world before he arrived in Philadelphia. Franklin became publisher of eight American editions of Whitefield's ongoing *Journals.* The Philadelphia printer also published quite a few of Whitefield's sermons and other writings. Franklin kept Whitefield in the news, often with front-page items in *The Pennsylvania Gazette,* which both promoted the evangelist and helped Franklin to solicit subscriptions for forthcoming Whitefield publications.

Franklin also came to like and admire Whitefield personally. Even though they were almost opposites in their views about orthodox Christian doctrine, they were in other respects two of a kind.

Each was an extraordinary example of a new type of self-made man that was emerging in the modern age. Each came from a middling background; each had succeeded spectacularly by mastering techniques of communication and by not being shy about self-assertion. Edwards, by contrast, despite some modern sensibility in publishing his account of the awakening, was born into his status, was formally deferential in his manner, and was of an altogether different type of character from the two meteoric personalities who first met in Philadelphia in 1739. Franklin and Whitefield both were sociable, outgoing, and ready to break with convention when practical concerns for their immediate projects demanded it.

Franklin also liked Whitefield because of the social benefits of the revivals. Each of these self-made men was determined that his own success should also serve a larger cause. The deeply pious Whitefield was committed first to serving God, but that also meant that he should serve his fellow creatures by bringing to them the gospel message — and the resulting conversions would change people's lives. Their good works would, in turn, result in social transformation. Sometimes Whitefield supported specific social causes. He founded an orphanage in Georgia, following the example of pietists in Germany. Franklin liked to tell the story that when attending one of Whitefield's sermons he had determined to put nothing in the collection, but that after several strokes of the preacher's oratory about the orphanage he not only emptied his pockets, but asked his neighbor for a loan so that he could give more. Franklin recognized that in a newly settled and often unruly society, any reformation in morals would be a benefit to all. Always alert and receptive to whatever worked, Franklin promoted revivals.

In June 1740, half a year after Whitefield's initial visit, for instance, Franklin celebrated the ongoing awakening in a report in his *Pennsylvania Gazette.* "The alteration in the fact of religion here is altogether surprising," he reported. "Surprising" was the term Edwards had used in the title to his *Faithful Narrative of the Surprising*

Work of God, and Franklin clearly echoed Edwards in making Philadelphia in 1740 sound almost like Northampton in 1735. "Religion is become the subject of most conversations. No books are in request but those of piety and devotion; and instead of idle songs and ballads, the people are everywhere entertaining themselves with psalms, and hymns, and spiritual songs."

While Franklin announced that all of this, "under God, is owing the successful labors of Mr. Whitefield," his account also reveals an aspect of the awakening which the concentration on its superstar has sometimes hidden. Whitefield had kindled and later rekindled revival fires in Philadelphia, but Franklin's June 1740 news report was about some of the other influential local evangelists who followed and sustained the awakenings. In this case Franklin was reporting on Presbyterians of the Middle Colonies who had gathered in Philadelphia for a meeting and who had used the occasion for preaching a series of fourteen sermons outdoors to "large audiences." Included in the lineup of Presbyterian evangelists were members of the Tennent family, the leading Scotch-Irish revivalists in the region. William Tennent Sr. and his sons William Jr. and Gilbert operated an influential "Log College" for ministerial training in the region. When Whitefield visited in 1739 and 1740 he was building on a revival base that such local preachers had already laid, and they in turn had adopted his methods of itinerant evangelism and outdoor preaching.

Hopes for the Future

A similar pattern developed in New England. In Northampton, Edwards had been discouraged about the cooling of revival fires since 1735, but he was also keeping track of every bit of news he could get of God's work elsewhere. Whenever a traveler arrived from Boston with a new supply of newspapers, Edwards eagerly searched them for news of revivals at home or abroad. In 1739 and 1740 White-field's visit to America put revivals much in the news. As soon as Edwards learned that Whitefield planned a trip to New England in 1740, he wrote to the young evangelist, urging him to come to Northampton. Whitefield had already written to Edwards suggesting the same.

Edwards warned the itinerant not to expect too much of New England. He feared that the formerly Puritan region, having "long enjoyed the gospel," might "have been glutted with it," making it a less promising place than elsewhere for Whitefield's labors. Knowing that Whitefield was familiar with Edwards's own renowned account of the "surprising work of God" in Northampton, Edwards probably wanted to lower expectations. Otherwise the contrast between the spiritually superheated town that Edwards had described in 1735 and the lukewarm Northampton that the evangelist might see in 1740 could prove embarrassing.

Despite his discouragements, ever since the awakening Edwards had worked mightily to help his congregation grow spiritually from the foundation of commitment that the awakening provided. The results were mixed. While he could still point to some transformed lives, the town as a whole had more or less slipped back to its old ways. Edwards was especially concerned about the return of bickering, contentions, and a bitter party spirit. Even a new meetinghouse became a source of conflict. In 1737 the town replaced the old unadorned Puritan meetinghouse with a handsome new steepled building (of the sort we associate with the "colonial style" of eighteenth-century New England). As was customary in hierarchical British colonial society, even church seating was assigned by rank. That inevitably led to squabbles in an American setting where economic factors changed the status of families over generations. Church members also wrangled over whether families should be seated together rather than seating men and women on different sides, as had been the custom until then. Eventually they decided to allow families to choose either way, but the whole process was less than edifying.

Edwards found the return of such petty town-wide controversies all the more disturbing because he believed that God had sent the town a dramatic warning. In the spring of 1737, as the new meeting-house was being built, the congregation was packed into the old building. The heaving from the spring thaw had shifted the building's foundations, and the crowded back gallery pulled out of its supports and fell down with a thunderous crash onto the area where women with small children were seated below. The "dolorous shrieking and crying" added to the terror, and everyone believed that many had been instantly killed. Yet when frantic parishioners pulled off the wreckage they found that, while many were cut and bruised, no one was killed — and not even a bone was broken. Nonetheless, as Edwards reported shortly after, this fearsome warning from God coupled with his miraculous show of mercy "had in no wise the effect that ten times less things were wont to have two or three years ago."

During these years after the awakening, as Edwards labored mightily to rekindle the spiritual fires, he preached two of what are now his best-known series of sermons. In "Charity and its Fruits," an engaging fifteen-part series delivered in the winter following the meetinghouse episodes, he closely followed the text of the famous biblical chapter on love in 1 Corinthians 13. True love or "charity," he affirmed, was the best evidence of genuine conversion and the opposite of the envy, quarrelling, and censoriousness that had reemerged in the town. In a second long series, "A History of the Work of Redemption," he situated the Northampton revivals within the whole panorama of the history of God's redemptive work. Starting in the Old Testament and carrying the story to the present, he emphasized that God's typical way of operating in history was through periodic outpourings of the Spirit in religious awakenings. He hoped that if the Northamptonites recognized that they had participated in one of the most remarkable spiritual outpourings since the Reformation, they might better appreciate and cultivate the work God had begun in them.

History was a tremendously important dimension of Edwards's thought. Late in his life he proposed to write an entire theology "in an entire new method, being thrown into the form of an history" called "A History of the Work of Redemption." Edwards's interest in trying to understand all of human experience through a historical lens anticipates in some ways outlooks typical of the modern age, but in other regards it challenges most modern views. Like more typically modern thinkers, Edwards was a firm believer in historical progress. In contrast to ancient views of history as cyclical, he believed that the world would improve at an accelerating rate. Unlike most moderns, however, he attributed this progress not to human improvement but to God's agency. God was moving history toward a grand redemptive culmination in a millennium (or thousand-year era) of spiritual outpourings, after which Jesus Christ would return at the time of the last judgment. This optimistic God-directed millennial expectation colored much of his outlook.

In the setting of the spiritual recession that followed the revival boom of 1734-35, his historical outlook both gave him extravagant hopes and braced him for some hard times along the way. Although he believed God ultimately controlled everything, he also saw that human history took place in an age in which God had, for mysterious reasons, permitted Satan to rebel and to rage against God's redemptive work. Human history thus was part of a larger cosmic warfare, in which people were lined up on one side or the other. Participating in a massive awakening was like being on the front lines of such a battle. A spiritual assault against Satan's rule in an awakening would be met by counterattacks until the day that Satan would eventually be defeated.

Still, even if Edwards had high hopes for the distant future and a good explanation for recent setbacks, he must have been disheartened by the spiritual downturn in Northampton. Physically, he was far from robust. We get a brief glimpse of this in 1739 when he was in Boston to give a public lecture and paid a courtesy call to his one-time mentor, Timothy Cutler, the former Yale rector who had turned Anglican. Cutler reported that Edwards was "very much emaciated, and impaired in his health, and it is doubtful to me whether he will attain the age of forty." Cutler attributed Edwards's condition to excessive study. In fact, his alarming appearance may have been related to an overly strict diet. Edwards often experimented with austere regimens that he believed improved his health and disposition. In addition, his condition could have been related to the recurrence of "melancholy" accompanied by physical weakness. The strain of the Northampton pastorate to which Edwards had dedicated so much of his energy in the past ten years doubtless had taken its toll.

Nonetheless, Edwards was driven by faith born of encounters with God's love and was filled with hope based on his reading of God's Word. And his faith was about to be rewarded. By the end of 1740, the visit of George Whitefield to New England would dramatically change Edwards's immediate prospects and put him near the center of a colonies-wide and international awakening that would transform the religious landscape and eventually have a profound political impact as well.

CHAPTER FIVE

An American Revolution

George Whitefield not only changed Jonathan Edwards's life; he changed American history. His influence was so great that he ought to be considered as one of America's leading founding fathers. One reason he is not, of course, is that he was not an American, but remained based in England, even though he visited America a remarkable seven times and died in Newburyport, Massachusetts, in 1771. Another reason why he is not as well remembered as others who shaped early America is that he was a religious figure, not a political one. Nonetheless, during his lifetime he was almost certainly the best-known person in the colonies, even more widely known among ordinary Americans than was his friend Benjamin Franklin. He was the first celebrated "star" in an emerging popular culture that, lacking hereditary aristocracy, would be particularly susceptible to stars. Not only was he famous: Whitefield revolutionized American religion, and hence much of American life.

Some of these same claims might be made for Edwards himself as a "founding father" who helped shape later American culture. He was the first to publicize revivals, he became their principal theorist, and he was long revered as the greatest theologian of revivalism, the nation's most influential theological tradition. Still, Edwards simply was not the revolutionary that Whitefield was.

Edwards was firmly planted as the authoritative pastor of an established, tax-supported church and never questioned the ancient assumption that authority should come from the top. A true revolution needed an outsider and an iconoclast, and Whitefield was perfect for the job.

The Great Awakening

Whitefield, even though he preached the same God-centered Calvinist theology Edwards did, was ready to break manmade rules if it meant serving God better. Particularly as a non-elite Anglican in England he had learned to operate outside of the conventional church — often literally outside while preaching in the fields. Soon he was moving toward a truly revolutionary pattern whenever he encountered opposition in the American colonies: he would appeal to the people *against* their pastors. That encouraged a dramatic reversal of roles. Traditionally pastors warned their congregations that they must change and become more spiritual and more moral. Now the traveling evangelist told people that they might be suffering spiritually because their pastors were spiritually dead. The blind were leading the blind. People who were truly awakened should challenge pastors who were not sufficiently spiritual. So it was that one principle of democracy — the authority of the common people — came to be realized in popular religion before it had widely emerged in the later politics of the American Revolution.

When Whitefield finally arrived in Boston in the fall of 1740, many of the clergy, despite some initial reservations, welcomed him. The city's leading pastor, Benjamin Colman, who had sponsored Edwards's narrative of the awakening, was among those who were especially supportive. Whitefield preached to unprecedented crowds of sometimes more than half the city's population of 17,000. After some weeks of preaching in the region, his farewell sermon in

Boston drew a crowd estimated between 23,000 and 30,000, or almost every able-bodied person in the greater Boston area.

From Boston the evangelist traveled by horseback some one hundred miles to the west to spend a weekend in Northampton. Whitefield and Edwards were immediately impressed by each other. They also made a sharp contrast. Edwards's gaunt appearance, exaggerated by his unusually tall frame of over six feet, must have made him appear older than his thirty-seven years. Whitefield, still only twenty-five, was robust, outgoing, energetic, and could hold a crowd spellbound simply by his eloquence. Yet they were united by their common Calvinist commitments and by their passion to save souls. Edwards felt that Whitefield hit just the right tone in chastising the Northamptonites for their backslidings. Whitefield recorded that "good Mr. Edwards wept during the whole time" of one of the Sabbath sermons. Many in the congregation were likewise reduced to tears. Whitefield wrote in his journal that he had not met the equal of Jonathan and Sarah Edwards in all New England.

Whitefield was charmed by the entire Edwards household. Jonathan asked him to meet with several of the older of their seven children; Sally was aged twelve, Jerusha was ten, Esther was eight, and Mary was six. Jonathan later reported that he saw a real work of God take place in them after that time. Whitefield found Sarah to be the model wife and mother. "A sweeter couple I have not seen," he wrote in his journal. "Mrs. Edwards is adorned with a meek and quiet spirit; she talked solidly of the things of God, and seemed to be such a helpmeet for her husband." After meeting Sarah, the young unmarried evangelist renewed his fervent prayers that God "would be pleased to send me a daughter of Abraham to be my wife."

When Whitefield left Northampton, Edwards accompanied him on horseback south for two days along the Connecticut River toward East Windsor, where Edwards's parents still lived. On the way Edwards got a taste of the immense potential of populist evangelism. Whitefield was a sensation wherever he went. In one famous account, a Connecticut farmer tells of literally dropping his plow at the news, grabbing his wife, and breathlessly racing, taking turns on their one horse, along with massive crowds, through clouds of dust, "as if we were fleeing for our lives, all the while fearing we should be too late to hear the Sermon."

Buoyed by his immense appeal to the people, Whitefield highlighted the democratic and subversive side of his message the more he traveled. Whereas in Northampton he was thoroughly supportive of Edwards, in many other places he challenged the authority of local pastors whom he judged to be insufficiently spiritual. Evangelical Protestantism has always used a certain language sprinkled with allusions to God's close presence and care along with one's concern for the salvation of souls. Whitefield and some of his fellow itinerants had become expert at quickly sizing up the many local clergy they encountered by the presence or absence of such language. Whitefield had included warnings about unconverted clergy in his preaching in Boston and did the same as he traveled the Connecticut River countryside. Edwards certainly agreed about the danger, but gently called Whitefield to task for making such quick judgments when only God knew the true state of someone's heart. Still, Whitefield persisted. In a journal that he would soon publish, he offended polite sensibilities by suggesting that many of New England's clergy were not truly Christian. Edwards must have had very mixed feelings about this publication, since Whitefield made his family a conspicuous exception. When they visited East Windsor together, Whitefield noted in his journal that the pastor there, Edwards's aged father Timothy, was "a converted man." In fact, Whitefield wrote that in the presence of Timothy and Esther Stoddard Edwards, "I fancied that I was sitting in the house of Zacharias and Elizabeth," the saintly old parents of John the Baptist in the New Testament.

In the two days that Edwards traveled with Whitefield he saw the beginnings of an American revolution, the emergence of the age of the people. Suddenly, official position or class carried no authority in religious matters unless one's soul was right with God. The simplest farmer who was converted could and should reject the authority of the most prestigious unregenerate clergyman. Edwards's work in the earlier awakening of 1734-35 had helped prepare the way for this revolution, but as an established clergyman who valued the authority of his office, he had not anticipated these wider consequences, even if he could appreciate their logic.

This revolution in authority was especially well suited to the American colonies. In America most established authorities were already weak, and most traditions were imported. Having almost no inherited nobility, colonists were already used to seeing enterprising men from modest backgrounds emerge as part of the ruling classes. Evangelicalism emphasized that anyone, no matter how humble in social or ecclesiastical status, might become a Spirit-filled son or daughter of God who would be spiritually superior to the most aristocratic of unregenerate men. For the moment few evangelicals (and certainly not Edwards) saw such spiritual equality as having implications for social status generally. But in the long run, the implications were there.

In the churches Whitefield was clearly challenging established authority, and his visit set off a chain reaction that was more immediately divisive. When Whitefield left New England, he asked Gilbert Tennent, one of his most enthusiastic and controversial supporters from the middle colonies, to succeed him in a New England tour. Early in 1740 Tennent had preached (and Benjamin Franklin had published) a sermon in Pennsylvania, "The Danger of an Unconverted Ministry," that was precipitating a schism among Presbyterians there. In December 1740 the fiery Presbyterian evangelist showed up in Boston to carry on Whitefield's work. Although Tennent was not as eloquent as Whitefield, his New England tour was remarkably successful in keeping the revival fires burning. His message also helped fuel controversy, and when Whitefield's journal was published the following spring, it too poured oil on the fires of both awakening and controversy.

For the time being there was no stopping the revival. Rather than relying on outsiders, many younger, pro-awakening New England clergy began itinerating themselves, crisscrossing the countryside preaching the awakening. Settled pastors were also finding that they were more likely to spark spiritual fervor if they ventured outside their own parishes. No one had seen an awakening of this size before. Even in Boston, pro-revival ministers reported unprecedented spiritual concerns and a seeming transformation of the city. This great awakening also grew dramatically in intensity. In response to revival preaching, people often cried out for the state of their souls, fainted, or were overcome by ecstasies.

Sinners in the Hands of an Angry God

Edwards seized the moment in a way that has been long remembered. Following the new trends of the revival, he altered his sermons to create more dramatic intensity and he began preaching more outside his own parish. That combination led to the most famous — or infamous — incident of his life: the preaching of "Sinners in the Hands of an Angry God" in Enfield, Connecticut.

The setting was a village near the border of Massachusetts and Connecticut in mid-July 1741. The next town, Suffield, had been experiencing an amazing revival for some time. On the Sunday three days before his Enfield sermon, Edwards, as a guest minister, presided over a communion service in Suffield in which an astonishing ninety-seven people were admitted as communicant members. The Suffield awakening had already produced intense ecstatic outbursts. On the Monday after the communion service, Edwards preached at a "private meeting" to a crowd packed into two large rooms of a house. A visitor who arrived after the sermon said that from a quarter-mile away he could hear howling, screeching, and groaning "as of women in the pains of childbirth" as people agonized over the states of their souls. Some fainted or were in trances; others were overcome with extraordinary bodily shaking. Edwards and others prayed with many of the distraught and brought some to "different degrees of peace and joy, some to rapture, all extolling the Lord Jesus Christ" and urged others to come to the Redeemer.

Two days later Edwards joined a group of visiting pastors who were trying to spread the revival to Enfield and was asked, no doubt with his success in Suffield in mind, to preach a sermon. Edwards was not like Whitefield, who could win over a congregation by free-wheeling dramatic eloquence. His voice was weak, and he preached from a full manuscript that he had virtually memorized. He used few gestures and made little eye contact. It was said that he seemed to be staring through the bell rope in the back of the church. Yet his sermons were a combination of luminously clear logic and spiritual intensity that could sometimes cast a spell over his listeners. In the case of "Sinners," unlike most of his sermons, he added extensive vivid imagery. The combination proved overwhelming.

"Sinners" is usually cited as an example of the harshness of hell-fire preaching in early America. But to see it as only that is to miss much of the point. Preachers of this era regularly preached on hell because they believed that it was a terrible reality about which people needed to be warned. They regarded the doctrine of eternal punishment as mysterious and horrifying, but Jesus himself had referred to it and most Christians in all eras had taken him literally. To alert one's parishioners to a real danger was a loving thing to do, and the more one could help them truly feel their peril, the more effective was the warning. Even preachers of a liberal sort used the doctrine of future rewards and punishments to help keep people in line morally. For conversionist-oriented Christians, more than morality was at stake: Evangelicals such as Edwards spoke of "awakenings" because people who were blinded by the pleasures of their sins needed to be awakened to their immense peril and God's remedy for it in Christ.

In Edwards's famous awakening sermon, he took the fires of hell for granted and placed central focus on the awful tension between God's judgment and God's mercy. Edwards presented God as the perfectly just judge who was righteously outraged at the rebellion of humans against his love. At the same time God mercifully held back for a time in carrying out his judgments, so as to give sinners a chance to receive Christ's redemptive love, to repent, and to be saved from an otherwise sure, just, and horrible condemnation.

Edwards built the overwhelming imagery of the sermon around God's long-restrained but impending wrath. "The black clouds of God's wrath [are] now hanging over your heads, full of the dreadful storm, and big with thunder." Or "like great waters that are damned for the present; they increase more and more, and rise higher and higher." Again, "the bow of God's wrath is bent, and the arrow made ready on the string, and justice bends the arrow at your heart, and strains the bow." So Edwards piled image upon image. Moreover, he drove home the point that it was not God's judgment or wrath that was at fault, but the essential sinfulness of each person that made that judgment just. "Your wickedness makes you as it were heavy as lead, and to tend downwards with great weight and pressure toward hell." "Unconverted men walk over the pit of hell on a rotten covering," and may fall through at any moment. Or in the most famous passage: "The God that holds you over the pit of hell, much as one holds a spider, or some other loathsome insect over a fire . . . 'tis nothing but his hand that holds you from falling into the fire every moment: 'tis to be ascribed to nothing else, that you did not go to hell last night" or "since you arose in the morning" or "since you have sat here in the house of God." "Oh sinner!" he pled. "Consider the fearful danger you are in . . . you hang by a slender thread, with the flames of divine wrath flashing about it, and ready every moment to singe it, and burn it asunder; and you have . . . nothing to lay hold of to save yourself . . . nothing that you can do, to induce God to spare you one moment."

Edwards never finished the sermon at Enfield. The tumult became too great as the audience was overcome by screaming, moanings, and crying out: "What shall I do to be saved. Oh I am going to Hell. Oh what shall I do for Christ?" One of the fellow ministers recorded that the "shrieks and cries were piercing and amazing." A number of "souls were hopefully wrought upon that night and oh the cheerfulness and pleasantness of their countenances."

The sermon and its effects were all the more frightening because the cacophony in the room prevented Edwards from getting to the part about God's mercy: "and now you have an extraordinary opportunity, a day wherein Christ has flung the door of mercy wide open, and stands in the door calling and crying with a loud voice to poor sinners." These were themes that Edwards often preached on in other sermons. In this one he had planned to remind his hearers of such a provision, of how many others had heard Christ's call with love and joy, and "how awful it is to be left behind at such a day!" His hearers, ironically, prevented him from getting to the good news he had come to bring.

Edwards could literally scare the hell out of an audience, but he also had a much gentler side. We get a glimpse of that caring pastoral quality in a letter of advice that Edwards wrote that same summer. Deborah Hathaway, an eighteen-year-old convert in the Suffield awakening, had turned to Edwards for counsel. So Edwards offered a list of guidelines for young Christians. At one time this letter was probably more widely known than "Sinners," since in the years before the American Civil War it was printed in great numbers as a tract titled *Advice to Young Converts*. In it Edwards emphasized the importance of humility and of not being discouraged. Young converts must trust in Christ to overcome persistent sins. Edwards's tone here offers a striking contrast to "Sinners in the Hands of an Angry God." The triune God is not only the terrifyingly righteous judge, but also the loving Christ, whose hands are gentle. "In all your course," Edwards urges, "walk with God and follow Christ as a little, poor, helpless child, taking hold of Christ's hand, keeping your eye on the mark of the wounds on his hands and side, whence came the blood that cleanses you from sin."

Defending the Awakening

Part of Edwards's concern in urging humility and gentle discipleship among converts was that, with extravagant outbursts now accompanying revivals all over New England, many people who might have otherwise been sympathetic were beginning to dismiss the awakenings as the contagion of sheer emotionalism. And Edwards himself worried that some people were using alleged conversion experiences to call attention to themselves and assert their spiritual superiority. Still, he had seen up close much of the anguish and ecstasies of converted sinners. Even taking into account the excesses and abuses of the awakenings, he was convinced that the benefits outweighed the risks.

He had a dramatic opportunity to address such issues as the speaker at the Yale commencement in September 1741. In all likelihood the Yale authorities had extended this honor to him before he became so involved in the outbursts of the summer. By the time he arrived in New Haven the controversy had broken into a storm, of which Yale was the epicenter. The conservative rector of the college, Thomas Clap, had at first welcomed the awakening. Visits by Whitefield in the fall of 1740 and by Gilbert Tennent in the spring had sparked revival fervor, and many in the college and the town seemed truly awakened. Later in the spring, however, when Whitefield published his *Journal,* it contained not only his observations regarding which New England ministers were or were not converted but also a scathing swipe at the college. Lumping Harvard and Yale together (much to the chagrin of the more conservative Yale), the evangelist lamented that "their light is become darkness, darkness that can be felt, and is complained of by the most godly ministers."

Far worse, some local traveling preachers, and even some Yale students, were saying the same thing. Just before the commencement the Yale trustees passed a regulation saying that "if any student of this college shall directly or indirectly say, that the rector, either of the trustees or tutors are hypocrites, carnal or unconverted men, he shall for the first offence make public confession in the hall, and for the second offence be expelled." One of the main targets was an intensely spiritual and outspoken student named David Brainerd. Eventually Yale expelled Brainerd after he was overheard to remark that one of the tutors "had no more grace than a chair."

Edwards could hardly have been prepared for the tempest he confronted in New Haven. The most controversial of all the evangelists, James Davenport, a descendent of the founder of the original New Haven colony, was in town for commencement week. Davenport had been whipping up enthusiasm among Connecticut audiences and telling them that their pastors' preaching was "to their souls, as rat bait is to their bodies." In New Haven he specifically attacked the Reverend Joseph Noyes of the town's First Church on the Green (where Yale students were required to attend) as a "wolf in sheep's clothing." Davenport's extravagant attacks created consternation among Yale authorities, but that won him all the more ardent admirers among students such as Brainerd.

If Rector Clap and the Yale Trustees hoped that Edwards would calm the storm, they must have been indignant about what he actually did. Whatever his reservations about some of its extravagant expressions, Edwards was unmistakably on the side of the awakening. Even if students like David Brainerd went too far in criticizing their superiors, Edwards admired their deep spiritual intensity. In his commencement address, soon published as an expanded treatise,

Edwards argued with his usually lucid logic that intense physical phenomena such as "tears, trembling, groans, loud outcries, agonies of body or the failing of bodily strength" did not prove anything one way or the other about the legitimacy of a revival. He did not think that a time of extraordinary gifts of the Holy Spirit had arrived, so he denied (contrary both to some radicals of his day and to later Pentecostals) that ecstatic signs were the best evidence of a true outpouring of the Holy Spirit. At the same time, he insisted, neither were overwhelming emotional outbursts evidences *against* the presence of the Holy Spirit. They might well be expressions entirely appropriate to the stupendous lifesaving character of what was happening. Crying out in fear of hell, for instance, made perfect sense. So also were ecstatic expressions of joy just what one might expect from those who authentically experienced the wonders of Christ's saving work.

True, Edwards recognized, there were dangers of excesses. Enthusiasm often spread even when evangelists proclaimed false doctrine. And Satan could simulate true awakenings. Still, such worst-case scenarios did not negate the fact that some of those overcome with extreme emotions in the revivals had been savingly converted. The real tests or "distinguishing marks" of a genuine work of the Spirit of God had nothing to do with such dramatic effects or the lack thereof. Rather, these tests were found in the changed lives of those who were now living according to the dictates of the gospel and manifested the traits and virtues of true Christians. Edwards had seen too many instances of such transformations to doubt that, on the whole, the awakening was a great outpouring of God's Spirit.

At the end of his discourse he did warn against some excesses — especially the habit of publicly declaring who is or is not truly converted. Since the first Northampton awakening Edwards had learned much about how easy it was to be wrong in judging external signs, and so he urged caution in evaluating others, especially those one did not know well. He also warned (as he had advised Whitefield) against the dangers of claiming to be led by God in making specific daily decisions by "impulses and strong impressions" of what God was telling one to do. Such, he feared, bordered on claims to extra-biblical revelations. Still, for Rector Clap and other Yale officials who may have hoped for calming moderation, this was too little, too late.

Edwards's central message was a sharp challenge to those who would dismiss the whole revival because of its evident excesses. If, as he said was demonstrable, the Holy Spirit had been working in remarkable ways in these revivals, then to oppose the revivals was to oppose the Holy Spirit. In Boston, where a backlash against the awakening was emerging, Edwards's pro-awakening friends published his treatise with an effusive preface by the Rev. William Cooper of the famed Brattle Street Church. Cooper went so far as to proclaim that the awakening had now surpassed the Reformation as the greatest spiritual outpouring since Pentecost. Both Cooper and Edwards suggested that those who opposed the awakening were in danger of "blasphemy against the Holy Spirit," which, they warned, could be what the New Testament meant by the "unpardonable sin."

This was a gauntlet thrown down, and the New England clergy quickly came to an all-out war of words between the "New Light" proponents of the awakening and its "Old Light" adversaries. Until 1742, most of those who opposed the awakenings had been reluctant to speak out, sensing that they were in the minority. But as extravagant claims and ecstatic behavior became ever more common, their case grew stronger.

Especially embarrassing to the friends of the awakening were the increasingly wild antics of James Davenport. In the spring of 1742, in response to the potential divisiveness of Davenport and some others, the Connecticut General Assembly passed a law banning itinerants unless a local parish had invited them. When Davenport promptly broke this law, the Assembly examined him and concluded that his rantings were so extreme that he was *"disturbed in the rational faculties of his mind,* and therefore to be pitied and compassionated." They sent him back to his parish on Long Island. Soon he was back in New England, more extreme than ever. In March 1743 things reached a frenzied peak at New London, on the Connecticut coast. There Davenport oversaw bonfires among a breakaway group of mostly young converts. On one day they burned books of Puritan divines to signal their freedom from mere tradition. The next day, turning to the problem of worldliness, he had people throw jewelry, wigs, and any attractive clothes on the fire. Apparently he himself offered the very pants he was wearing. At that point some New Light friends stepped in, believing that he might be possessed of the devil.

Edwards played an important role in the sequel. He and a number of other leading New Lights met with Davenport, and afterward Edwards was among those who continued to counsel him. By the next year Edwards reported that the young evangelist was "truly very much altered." Davenport confessed his faults and acknowledged that he had been led by a "false Spirit," especially regarding the book and clothes burnings in New London. Although Davenport was restored, the damage had been done, as his extravagances had stoked the fires of anti-awakening reaction.

Charles Chauncy (1705-1787), junior pastor of Boston's prestigious First Church, emerged as the chief spokesman for the Old Lights. Chauncy later became known as something of a theological liberal who criticized some doctrines of Calvinism, but at this time he presented his argument in an orthodox framework. He was not against truly transformative works of the Holy Spirit, but he believed that these were usually manifested as a gradual process of recognizing and living according to God's grace. "Enthusiasm," as he called excessive displays of emotion, was a sort of overheated and contagious mental state that led people to mistake their own overwrought passions for a work of God. Such emotions were notoriously unreliable as guides for sorting out true religion from delusions. "The plain truth is," Chauncy insisted, "an *enlightened mind,* not *raised affections,* ought always be the guide of those who call themselves men; and this, in the affairs of religion, as well as other things."

Chauncy spoke out forcefully in the summer of 1742 and also let it be known that he was collecting materials for a major volume that would document the awakening's excesses. Edwards, meanwhile, must have been working in all his spare time to beat Chauncy to the punch, and in the spring of 1743 he came out with his own lengthy treatise, *Some Thoughts Concerning the Present Revival of Religion.* As in his earlier defense of the awakening, Edwards conceded that there were excesses, but he argued that these should not distract from the central evidences that the Holy Spirit was changing people's hearts. At about the same time Edwards's treatise appeared, the Reverend Thomas Prince, one of Boston's most distinguished clergymen and a close ally of Edwards, inaugurated a new periodical, *Christian History.* Following the example of a Scottish journal that was promoting similar revivals in Scotland, *Christian History* published accounts of impressive spiritual experiences taking place in the international awakenings.

By now New England's clergy were so sharply divided into two contending camps that almost everyone was forced to take sides. In the spring of 1743 a group of about forty Massachusetts clergy managed a minor coup. Sensing that they had a majority at an annual ministerial gathering in Boston, they issued a declaration condemning the most notorious disorders of the awakenings, including claims of direct leading of the Lord, judgments about who was converted, preaching by laypeople who were not properly educated, pandemonium in religious meetings, and separation from parish churches. Although the New Light clergy who were present, including Edwards, could agree on these dangers, they opposed this declaration since it lacked a positive affirmation of the genuine benefits of the awakening. Two months later, at another annual gathering of clergy at the time of the Harvard commencement in July, the New

Lights organized their own convention and issued a *Testimony and Advice* praising the awakening while also acknowledging its excesses. More than a hundred New England clergy eventually signed.

The war of words and of numbers continued. In September 1743, Charles Chauncy's tome appeared, over four hundred pages long, in answer to Edwards. It included more than five hundred subscribers of not only clergy but also what one historian described as the "social register" of laypeople of the region, headed by the Massachusetts governor, William Shirley.

Looking at this divide in terms of American colonial political and social history, we can see the revolutionary implications of what Whitefield brought to New England. For a century New England clergy and social elites had been able to present a remarkably solid front in maintaining the "New England Way," in which Calvinist religion and good social order went hand in hand. Upstart voices faced a hard time gaining a hearing, as had been perhaps best illustrated only twenty years earlier, when clergy and social-political elites could shut down the dissenting voice of James Franklin's *New England Courant.* The awakening brought an end to any such top-down governing consensus in religious matters. Laypeople could now criticize clergy with impunity — and even the clergy themselves were now publicly at each other's throats.

Edwards, who had been born into New England's establishment, was not entirely happy with the revolution he had helped precipitate in the region's churches. Although he strongly believed in the spiritual equality of all who were regenerate, whether male or female, slave or free, he also firmly held that church people should give due deference to the clergymen whom God had ordained. These were the men who were trained in biblical languages and the authoritative theology of the Protestant Reformation. So, for example, while he was happy to see laypeople testifying to their faith, he did not think that they should take up preaching unless they were properly trained.

While Edwards advised a number of untrained New Light laymen not to engage in formal preaching, he was even unhappier
when some women took it on themselves to exhort or preach. Edwards, in accord with the vast majority of Christians through most
of history, believed that women preaching, at least in mixed male
and female gatherings, violated a direct New Testament prohibi-
tion. The one instance in which we know he dealt directly with such
a matter provides a fascinating glimpse at the times. Early in 1742
Edwards sat on a visiting ministerial council dealing with a case in
Westfield, Massachusetts, of Bathsheba Kingsley, a radical New
Light, whose husband complained that she was spending almost all
her time away from home wandering from house to house to deliver
Christ's message of salvation. Earlier she had confessed to stealing
a horse in her zeal to evangelize a neighboring town. The council
treated her much the way a similar group had dealt with James Davenport, declaring her of an unstable character and aiming at reha-
bilitation rather than punishment. But this case added the issue of
gender. They said that she might continue to witness as proper to
"her station," which meant essentially at home, in private, or as an
invited guest to other homes. Also, they advised that she not criticize
her husband with rough or severe language, but "privately in an
humble submissive loving manner." He in turn should "treat her
with patience and gentleness without hard words or blows."

A Treatise Concerning Religious Affections

By the spring of 1743, Edwards's views of the awakening were mod-
erating. He seemed as much distressed by some of the radical New
Lights as he was by opponents of the awakening. In a letter written
in May 1743 he revealed his concern to the Reverend James Robe of
Kilsyth, Scotland, where there had been an amazing revival that was
part of a larger Scottish awakening. While Edwards rejoiced in the

news from Scotland, he declared that "wc have not such joyful news to send you; the clouds have thickened, especially in the division of New England into contending parties." "This is," Edwards explained, "very much owing to imprudent management in the friends of the work, and a corrupt mixture which Satan has found means to introduce, and our manifold sinful errors, by which we have grieved and quenched the Spirit of God."

By this time many of New England's towns had already been divided, as New Light churches broke off and formed their own congregations, usually basing their actions on accusations that the local Old Light pastor was unregenerate. Even though Edwards sided with the New Lights, he remained reluctant to endorse either such personal judgments or rejections of duly constituted authority. In dealing with such issues, he usually counseled charity on both sides. But charity was becoming a rare commodity.

Edwards's efforts to find a middle way in the awakening and to promote charity rather than acrimonious divisions culminated in one of his greatest works, *A Treatise Concerning Religious Affections,* published in 1746. This work was not simply another answer to Chauncy and the Old Lights; rather, it was a more positive attempt to strike a balance by offering ground rules on how to resolve the contested issues about what constituted true Christianity. It was addressed as much to the New Lights as to opponents of the awakening.

Edwards emphasized in his preface that often more damage was done to true religion by its avowed friends then by its announced foes. One of Satan's favorite strategies was to simulate genuine religious experiences in extreme ways that were caricatures of the real thing, hence discrediting the whole. Edwards had by this time seen many cases in Northampton in which he had thought parishioners were genuinely converted, only to see them backslide in subsequent years. True converts proved to be like fixed stars, while imitation conversions were more like comets that blazed brightly for a while but eventually burned out. The central problem that Edwards addressed in *Religious Affections* was how to tell these two types apart.

Edwards began by once again defending the centrality of deeply felt affections. "True religion," he set forth as an opening thesis, "in great part consists in holy affections." These affections were what a person truly loved, and these loves inevitably guided the will in its choices. Genuine faith in Scripture was not just a matter of believing in right doctrine, though correct belief was certainly necessary. Rather, true religion centered in heartfelt affections "such as fear, hope, love, hatred, desire, joy, sorrow, gratitude, compassion and zeal." Since these feelings were responses to the amazing love of God, who in Christ would suffer on behalf of contemptible sinners, it should be no surprise that these emotions might sometimes be overwhelming. Extreme emotions and accompanying physical effects were not necessarily evidences of false experiences that would prove short-lived.

Yet how could one tell? Edwards had seen many cases in which supposed converts were swept into contagious enthusiasm but in the long run did not change their ways. He had also seen cases, sometimes longer lasting, in which such converts seemed to be more in love with their own experience than with God, more proud of their new spiritual status than changed in their hearts. Edwards's concerns about such abuses were one thing he had in mind when he warned against quick judgments about the states of others' souls. When he advised converts, as in the case of young Deborah Hathaway, he typically underscored that they should display deep humility. Knowing the deceitfulness of the human heart as he did — and no doubt reflecting insight on his own struggles — he also warned that pride could disguise itself as excessive humility. Sometimes people deceived even themselves.

In the light of these complexities, Edwards attempted in *Religious Affections* to provide some guidelines for distinguishing between true and false religion. Only God, he emphasized, could know the true state of someone's heart. Any tests we might devise would still leave some uncertainty. Nevertheless, Scripture revealed many *signs* of true faith, and Edwards presented what he hoped would be a definitive list of twelve such signs. Those who believed God was working in their hearts could use these signs as guides to true Christian living.

A number of these signs had to do with Edwards's central emphasis that true religious experience had to focus on God's excellencies rather than on oneself. The very essence of Christian experience was to have a truly affecting sense of the love and beauty of God, most fully revealed in Christ's sacrifice. Such gratitude, if truly heartfelt, would draw one out of selfishness into loving God and others. Other signs had to do with "Christ-like" qualities such as a "lamb-like" or "dove-like" demeanor and what the New Testament calls "fruits of the Spirit," such as patience, kindness, and gentleness. The final and culminating sign was that true affections would result in true Christian practice.

As in most religious traditions, good works were essential for true followers. Of course, as a Calvinist, Edwards also made clear that one was not saved by good works or by following a set of rules. Nonetheless, good works were tremendously important as the best test of true faith. If one's strongest affections or loves were absorbed in love to God, then good works, showing that one loved what God loved, would follow. If good works were few, chances were the faith was not genuine.

By 1746, when *Religious Affections* appeared, Edwards had positioned himself solidly between the two extremes regarding the Great Awakening and defined a position for moderate evangelicalism. He was one of the strongest supporters of the revivals, but he held firm in challenging its excesses and the superficialities of temporary enthusiasms. Awakenings, he insisted, must be tested by the long-term affections and behaviors they generated. That concern, which had matured greatly since his own early enthusiasm of the awakening of 1734-35, arose most particularly out of his experiences in the meantime in the volatile town of Northampton.

Joseph Badger, *Reverend Jonathan Edwards (1703-1758) B.A. 1720, M.A. 1723.*

Courtesy Yale University Art Gallery, Bequest of Eugene Phelps Edwards.

Robert Feke, *Portrait of Benjamin Franklin* (1746), one of the few portraits available of Franklin as a young man.

Courtesy Harvard University Art Museum, Fogg Art Museum,
Harvard University Portrait Collection, Bequest of Dr. John Collins Warren, 1856, H47.

Joseph Badger, *Mrs. Jonathan Edwards (Sarah Pierpont).*
Courtesy Yale University Art Gallery, Bequest of Eugene Phelps Edwards.

Late eighteenth-century Northampton as conceived by
twentieth-century artist Maitland de Gorgoza.

Courtesy the Forbes Library, Northampton, Massachusetts.

PREACHING TO SOLDIERS.

"As many as were in debt came to David, and he became captain over them."

George Whitefield preaching to soldiers in Boston.

Illustration in John Gillies, *Memoirs of Rev. George Whitefield* (Hartford, Connecticut: E. Hunt, 1853).

Jonathan Edwards's desk with later bookcases, 1700–1730. He added on to the original desk to provide more space for his work.

Courtesy Yale University Art Gallery.

The Mission House, Stockbridge, Massachusetts,
home of Abigail Williams Sergeant Dwight, Edwards's rival.

Photo courtesy the Trustees of Reservations.

A North West Prospect of Nassau-Hall, with a Front View of the President's House, in New Jersey.

Nassau Hall and the president's house, Princeton, where Edwards died.
Illustration by Henry Dawkins.

CHAPTER SIX

Drama on the Home Front

—⟨⟨⟨⟨∅∅∅⟩⟩⟩⟩—

Edwards's role in the awakenings put him on a world stage, but the most poignant scenes of his life were played out in a small frontier town and in the midst of a large family. During the 1740s his sometimes-extravagant hopes for the awakenings were tempered by the realities of his often-contentious parishioners. In the 1730s Northampton became internationally renowned, but it was the decade from 1740 to 1750 that proved the most dramatic in the town's history. Beginning with the spiritual high following Whitefield's visit, it would end with Edwards's dismissal from his pastorate. In the meantime the town was the scene for a wide range of human struggles, from the grand to the petty. And the large Edwards family (their eleventh child was born in 1750) was beginning to come of age. During the turbulent decade of the 1740s they would experience spiritual ecstasy, love, warfare, Indian threats, sacrifice, death, conflict, and rejection.

Almost as soon as Whitefield left Northampton in October 1740, Edwards launched a campaign to avoid a repeat of what had happened after the 1734-35 awakening, when many Northamptonites drifted away from the revival fervor. Whitefield's preaching had left the congregation in tears, but Edwards had seen such tears before and feared another round of "false conversions." Soon after Whitefield's departure Edwards delivered a series of nine sermons (churches held two services each Sabbath, morning and afternoon) on the "Parable of the Sower" from Matthew 13. In Jesus' story the sower cast seed, which represented the preaching of the gospel. Some fell by the wayside and was devoured by birds. Some fell on stony ground and sprang up quickly, but died from lack of root. Some fell on thorny ground and grew but was eventually choked by weeds. Others fell on good ground and brought forth much fruit. The main thrust of the sermon series was to chastise those Northamptonites who fit into the first three categories. Some were so hardened that Edwards said he would "rather preach to the men of Sodom" than to them. Others, in the second and third categories, were hypocrites who responded emotionally to a preacher like Whitefield, but whose superficial faith would not bear fruit in the long run.

Whatever the effects on those who knew themselves to be the targets of these admonitions, by the spring another revival was underway, especially among the young people. This time the awakening was part of the "Great Awakening" that was sweeping over all of New England as well as the other British-American colonies. Once again Edwards met with young people and children in private meetings in various houses. This time, however, as was happening elsewhere, the responses in outcries and physical effects were much more extravagant. The summer was the same one in which Edwards's "Sinners in the Hands of an Angry God" triggered convulsions of fear and joy in Enfield like he had already been seeing at home, first among young people and then spreading to others. Some smaller group meetings in homes became immensely intense. Many would cry out, some would faint, and others would be overwhelmed by strong physical reactions. In some evening meetings people were so overcome physically that they had to stay overnight.

The Edwards Family and Their Town

Seeing these ecstatic outbursts among people whom he knew so well must have been one of the things that had convinced Edwards to defend the Great Awakening so vigorously, even though he was all too aware, from the earlier Northampton awakening, of the deceptiveness of heightened emotions. One personal factor renewing his hopes was that his own children were involved. His daughters Sally, Jerusha, and Esther were ages thirteen, eleven, and nine respectively by the end of 1741. Already, shortly after Whitefield left in 1740, Edwards wrote excitedly that he hoped salvation had come "to one, if not more, of my children" in the aftermath of the evangelist's visit. Jerusha soon became especially known as a model of spirituality.

Sarah Edwards, who herself had been spiritually precocious when Jonathan first admired her as a young girl singing to God in the fields, was now at least as much as Jonathan a spiritual example to the family. Our best glimpses of Sarah and her spirituality come from the winter of 1741-42, as Northampton's involvement in the Great Awakening continued to intensify. It happened that in December 1741 Samuel Hopkins, a twenty-two-year-old Yale graduate and admirer of Jonathan, came to stay at the Edwards home. Hopkins himself would become a major theologian as well as the first biographer of Edwards. In 1741 he was a shy student, dejected because he was not finding the intense experience that his fellows found in the awakening. As though Sarah did not already have enough to do, the Edwardses took in a succession of such students who wanted to study with Jonathan. Yet Sarah soon drew Hopkins out of his misery. She provided him "light and comfort" and assured him that she believed "God intended yet to do great things by me, etc." Hopkins later wrote: "She would spare no pains to make [visitors] welcome and provide for their convenience and comfort. And she was peculiarly kind to strangers who came to her house."

Sarah's household duties were overwhelming at times, and it is no wonder that Jonathan reported that, despite her outgoing warm manner to others, she could experience extended times of melancholy. Eighteenth-century households, such as the Edwardses', were not divided strictly into "separate spheres" in the way of the middle classes of the later Victorian era when women, despite many domestic duties, were often considered delicate and to be sheltered. Even an elite home such as the Edwardses' reflected something closer to a farm economy. Northampton house lots included plots for gardening, and part of the pastor's reimbursement came from farming one of the many tracts that surrounded the town. In the Edwardses' situation, with Jonathan working all day in his study, Sarah acted as a sort of "deputy husband." Not only did she oversee the house, the meals, and her many children; she also watched over servants (including an African woman slave — of which more later) and the farming operations. Hopkins remarked that Jonathan seldom knew how many animals they owned, whereas Sarah kept oversight over the whole operation. Sarah managed all this while she was almost always either nursing an infant or pregnant. Samuel Hopkins reported that in caring for her many children, Sarah was careful to break the will at the first sign of obstinacy, but she always disciplined "with all calmness and gentleness of mind." According to the admiring Hopkins, the "quarrelling and contention" that one often sees among children "was not known among them."

In January 1742, when the Great Awakening in New England reached its peak, Sarah experienced a time of amazing spiritual ecstasy. Jonathan was going out of town for two weeks to preach in other churches, and the Edwards home was overflowing with a constant stream of guests. Various neighboring ministers and itinerants came to stoke the Northampton revival fires in a series of meetings while Jonathan was gone.

Sarah was sensitive about what the townspeople said about Jonathan. Pastors' salaries were negotiated every year in town meetings, and Edwards often pointed out that his income was not keeping up with inflation. Townspeople said the family spent too much, citing Sarah's taste in clothes and even an occasional modest bit of jewelry. Townspeople were also quick to criticize Jonathan. Sarah was particularly sensitive to whispers that a visiting preacher had more success than did her husband. Sarah could also be devastated by any disapproval from Jonathan, and she was recently distressed by his mild criticism of something she had said to one of the guest pastors. Sarah viewed all these sensitivities and jealousies as faults on her part and prayed mightily to God for grace to overcome them.

In the midst of these struggles, and at a gathering with houseguests for mid-morning prayers, Sarah suddenly found herself able to submit her will entirely to God. She was overcome with a euphoria and sense of peace that "was altogether inexpressible." Amazingly, these raptures continued and increased over the next two weeks, so that Sarah experienced a sort of "heavenly Elysium" or "ravishing sense of the unspeakable joys of the upper world." During these days she often was overcome physically, so that she might involuntarily rise up out of her chair or feel so spiritually transported that she would fall into a swoon. Amid this spiritual euphoria, she continued cheerfully to perform her household duties. When during the second week a particularly fervent young evangelist, twenty-five year-old Samuel Buell, preached with great effect at a midweek service, not only did Sarah find herself free of jealousy at his success, but also she herself was among the many moved by his fiery preaching. Physically overcome, she remained at the meetinghouse for three hours conversing with others on spiritual things. She felt so submitted to God's will, and so overcome by his grace, that she believed she could accept anything, even disaster for her family, abuse, or martyrdom.

When Jonathan returned he was delighted to hear of Sarah's ecstasies, so much so that he copied down a full account, which she dictated. In his lengthy defense of the awakenings, *Some Thoughts Concerning the Present Revival of Religion in New England,* published in the fall of 1742, he included a version of her story, but he disguised her identity and gender. This experience, he argued, was conclusive evidence that the extreme fervors and ecstasies of the awakenings could not be dismissed as merely the experiences of immature people infected by some "distemper catched from Mr. Whitefield or Mr. Tennent." Rather, he testified, this was one of the most mature and proven Christians he had ever met. After fifteen years of marriage, Jonathan still admired Sarah as a spiritual model as much as he had when she was a girl. "If this be distraction," he proclaimed, "I pray God that the world of mankind may be all seized with this benign, meek, beneficient, beatifical, glorious distraction!"

Edwards also found the townspeople under Buell's temporary ministry in a state of religious commotion that in some ways surpassed anything they had experienced before. Some very radical New Lights from Suffield had accompanied Buell, and they were apparently exciting some townspeople to extremes. Even while Edwards was so pleased with Sarah's state of ecstasy, he found the heated emotions of some others alarming. The effect of the revival was not so much in new conversions as in extreme experiences by those already professing. For many these manifestations were "far beyond" anything they experienced before. Some fell into motionless trances for twenty-four hours at a time. Others felt they had been transported to heaven and were seeing glorious visions. It soon became apparent, Edwards later wrote, that "Satan took advantage" of these people. Probably they were engaging in extra-biblical prophecies and claims of messages from God, condemnations of others, and the like. In any case, Buell remained with Edwards for two or three weeks as they labored to keep many of the people from "running wild."

Edwards also tried to turn the fervor of revival into something permanent by combining it with an even older American religious institution: the public covenant. The Puritan founders had placed great emphasis on covenants, which were based on Old Testament models of contractual promises between God and Israel. In response to God's promise to care for his faithful people, the people promised to obey God, especially by following his commands. In March 1742, while the town was still in an excited state, Edwards led them in a solemn ceremony renewing their covenant with God.

In the covenant that Edwards drew up for Northampton, the townspeople promised to keep from their old wicked ways. Edwards was trying to avoid a repetition of the backsliding he had seen after the earlier awakening. In the midst of their spiritual enthusiasm he had them promise in great detail how they would pursue strict rules of honesty, justice, and uprightness, not defrauding each other, not bickering and fighting, but always treating each other with charity, or the law of love. Young people pledged to avoid meeting and diversions that would distract from religion or excite lusts. Everyone vowed to work hard at their religious duties. Recognizing that these resolves would be tested by their continuing sinful inclinations, they promised faithfully to examine themselves and to renew their covenant, especially before each monthly celebration of the Lord's Supper.

Edwards remained immensely hopeful about the awakenings that were reverberating throughout the colonies early in 1742. In *Some Thoughts Concerning the Present Revival,* which he finished around that spring, he even went so far as to remark that the awakenings might be "the dawning, or at least a prelude, of that glorious work of God, so often foretold in Scripture, which in the progress and issue of it, shall renew the world of mankind." Readers would know that he was referring to the coming of the millennium, which many Christians believed would be a wonderful thousand-year era at the end of human history. Edwards, like many Protestant Bible interpreters of his time, believed that after this culminating golden age Jesus Christ would return in judgment, followed by a new heaven and a new earth. Though Edwards did not fully explain his views in *Some Thoughts,* he believed that the beginning of the millennium was some time off (perhaps starting around A.D. 2000) and that in the meantime there would be both great spiritual advances for the church and also many trials, wars, and persecutions as Satan fought back. So by "the dawning, or at least a prelude," he meant something like the glimmers of light seen before a day actually started. Still, he held a very optimistic view of where human history was headed, and he maintained an exceedingly high estimate of the significance of the revival as a turning point in that history.

Edwards's remark about "the dawning, or at least a prelude, of that glorious work of God" might not have attracted much notice had he not added a further comment that "there are many things that make it probable that this work will begin in America." A number of his readers, including friends such as the celebrated author and hymn writer Isaac Watts in England, criticized him for this high estimate of America's destiny. Edwards soon regretted the remark and disavowed it. By the mid 1740s the awakening would look very different to him, especially as he viewed it through his experience in Northampton.

A Visionary and a Natural Aristocrat

Edwards's changing relationship to his parishioners in Northampton provides us with the best opportunity to reflect on what sort of person Edwards was. He was a passionate visionary, a world-class intellectual, and an intense ascetic who lived in a very real world of a large energetic family and a volatile and often contentious village. As a visionary, he had the ability to inspire people, especially in the revival of 1734-35, when he seemed to have virtually the whole town affectionately listening to him. During the Great Awakening of 1741-42 he once again gained a wide hearing, though probably with a little more dissent this time. Even though Edwards might appear to have been austere, he seems to have had some of his best success working in smaller groups and with young people. His intensity and crystal-clear logic seems to have been combined with a warmth of genuine concern that got through to many people.

Driven by his theological vision that a loving, faithful relationship to God was by far the most important thing in life and that all other loves had to be subordinate to that, Edwards set a standard of faith and practice that was difficult for most people to sustain. He himself was extraordinarily disciplined spiritually. He spent much time in regular prayers both privately and at set times daily with his family. He was said to spend thirteen hours a day in his study. Such an exhausting regimen reflected both an extraordinary work ethic and intense spiritual discipline. He strictly regulated his diet, which he believed helped him work more effectively and preserve his delicate health. He lived almost like a monk in the midst of a busy world. For breaks he might chop wood in the winter or ride in the summer into the countryside for reflection and spiritual contemplation. Not wishing to waste any time but finding it difficult to carry quill and ink, he would pin bits of paper to his jacket to remind him later to write down his most useful thoughts. He could sustain the highest standards of discipline for himself. But these standards could be daunting to others.

Edwards knew that he was not good at small-talk in social situations. Partly for that reason, he did not make many routine pastoral calls on the members of his congregation. He felt that his time was better spent in his study, although during revivals parishioners often lined up to see him there. His student and biographer, Samuel Hopkins, insisted that the accusation that Edwards was *"stiff* and *unsociable"* was groundless, but many people found him so. Hopkins countered that among his friends, when talking on serious subjects, he was an animated conversationalist. Both the accusation and the counter were likely true. Anyone who shared his deep theological and spiritual concerns would find Edwards fascinating to be with; those who did not would see him as too serious and intimidating.

88

To understand and appreciate Edwards, we also have to take into account how different some things were that his society took for granted, especially regarding hierarchy and equality, as compared with the western world today. The story of Rip Van Winkle reminds us of how much the world would have seemed turned upside down if someone had slept through the American Revolution. Edwards, who died in 1758, lived entirely before that dramatic era of change and before new ideas of social equality became widespread. He was a British citizen who took for granted very British ideas of social hierarchy and deference. The colonies had very few titled aristocracy, but they did have what John Adams and Thomas Jefferson later agreed might be called a "natural aristocracy." In New England that included not only "gentlemen" who might serve as judges and magistrates, but also clergy, who commanded special respect in this religiously shaped culture. Edwards assumed that these two elite groups should cooperate closely. In Northampton he made common cause with his uncle, Colonel John Stoddard, who was a faithful churchman, a military leader, a sort of squire of the town, and also the person most often elected to represent Northampton in the colonial legislature or appointed as regional judge.

Slavery

Edwards's eighteenth-century society was thoroughly patriarchal. At that time, "patriarchy," or fatherly rule and care, was considered a matter of common sense, and to provide such rule and care was considered virtuous. Most people depended for their welfare on personal relationships and particularly their relationships with their immediate social superiors. Ideally these relationships should be like that of a father and a family. The father held all the authority, but should rule lovingly. In marriage, for instance, most people found it almost unthinkable that husband and wife should be equal.

89

Who would be in charge? It seemed obvious that in all of nature and society God had ordained some to be stronger and some weaker. Subordinates should depend on their superiors, and superiors should care for those whom God had entrusted to them.

It is in this context that we must try to understand how it was that almost everybody at this time still took slavery for granted as a social institution. Even most Africans did not oppose slavery or the slave trade in principle; their societies participated in both. Nonetheless, Africans certainly resented the cruel, inhumane ways that slavery and the slave trade were practiced in the European context, especially since Africans were singled out for the worst kinds of slavery. Europeans, including the American colonists, did not see that distinction; for them, the institution of slavery was simply as old as human memory. Many people, including peasants or serfs on a noble's land, many indentured servants, captives in wars, and prisoners, worked more or less involuntarily and in subjection to their masters. The Bible did not condemn slavery as such. Only recently had the modern institution of *racially* based enslavement of Africans arisen. With it came the cruelties of the brutal slave trade, driven by the capitalist principle of finding the most efficient means to turn a profit. In the interlocking trade systems that shaped the Atlantic world, the economies of the American colonies soon were deeply enmeshed in a network of exchange that treated Africans as commodities. But most colonists saw this only as an evolution in the longstanding practice of slavery, not a cruel revolution.

Prior to the era of the American Revolution only the tiniest minority of colonists spoke out against slavery as such, even if many more became uncomfortable with some of the ways it was practiced. Benjamin Franklin, for instance, owned slaves during this era and in his newspapers advertised slaves for sale and ran ads for the return of runaways. Only later during the American Revolution did he speak out against slavery and the slave trade. Once Americans began to think of themselves as enslaved by Great Britain, many could recognize the analogous plight of African slaves. Franklin lived through what appeared to be largely a generational change of heart; Edwards's son, Jonathan Edwards Jr., and Edwards's closest disciple, Samuel Hopkins, became outspoken antislavery advocates in the revolutionary era. But in Edwards's own day it still seemed to most people very strange indeed to say that buying and owning slaves was in itself wrong. Many pious people reasoned that individual slaves whom they might purchase would be relatively better off as members of a good household.

Jonathan and Sarah Edwards seem to have usually owned one female household slave. We do know that one of these women, Leah, became a communicant church member during the revival of 1734-35. In all the awakenings it was common to find a few Africans and Indians included among the converts. Edwards held that all peoples are "of the same human race," and that this provided a reason against "the master's abuse of his servant." Although he believed that people who came from non-Christian cultures suffered from religious deficiencies, he thought that one day, as the gospel spread and the millennium approached, there would be great African and Native American theologians. Once they were part of the church, Africans and Indians were to be treated as spiritual equals. African and Indian men even seem to have been allowed to vote in church meetings. Spiritual equality, however, did not imply social equality. New England, like the rest of the western world, was as hierarchical as the military is today. Church seating, for instance, was determined by social rank.

Edwards recorded his views of slavery and the slave trade just once, and only in fragmentary notes that he jotted down, apparently for a meeting. Sometime late in 1741 Edwards was called to a ministerial council in response to a dispute between parishioners and the minister of a neighboring town. Some parishioners had criticized the minister for, among other things, owning slaves. In this era when white New Englanders almost never questioned the legitimacy of slavery, Edwards found the accusation so unusual that he believed it to be frivolous, only raised to cause trouble. Almost always inclined to defend authority, Edwards noted how one might respond to such an accusation. The Bible certainly allowed for slavery as it was practiced in the ancient world. At the same time, Edwards recognized that there was no biblical justification for the current practice of Europeans enslaving any dark-skinned African they could obtain, thereby putting his finger on the critical new issue in modern slavery. As a result, he was coming to the realization that the slave trade was wrong. But he was not enough of a revolutionary to propose abolishing an entire socioeconomic system. In the Edwards family, such a call would have to come from the next generation.

Rebels without (Much of) a Cause

In Northampton, Edwards's instinct to support traditional authority was beginning to put him out of step with an emerging younger American culture in which many would question the old hierarchies. Edwards had inherited from Solomon Stoddard a tradition of ministerial dominance over the town. Such authority, which he worked to preserve, accentuated a dual role Protestant pastors had to play. He was simultaneously the minister of the gospel who proclaimed the doctrines of grace and also, as the chief officer of the church, the person in charge of overseeing enforcement of church law. Since in Northampton the church and the town were more or less co-extensive, his role as chief disciplinarian of the church encompassed a major social dimension. In theory law and grace were to complement each other, but in practice the way a minister dealt with an offender could harden the parishioner against the gospel remedies and cause resentments throughout the town.

In Edwards's case, such tensions led to one of the most bizarre and damaging incidents of his ministry. In March 1744, just two years after the revival had been at its height, Edwards found out that for quite a while some young men had been passing around a couple of books for their sexual content. The books themselves were hardly scandalous. One was merely a text on midwifery. The other was a popular British publication that was a pseudo-scientific manual of information on human anatomy and sexuality, with a mildly titillating overtone. This incident is usually known as the "bad book" episode, but in fact Edwards's concern was not about the books, but rather about how they were being used: some of the young men involved were using information in these books to harass girls and to tease them about their menstrual cycles and other sexual matters.

Edwards would not have regarded crude joking about sexual matters or about these books as anything more than the petty incidents that they seem, except for two things. First, this matter had taken on a *public* dimension. It was not just young men talking dirty behind the barn; they were coarsely teasing young women. In the eighteenth century the term "sexual harassment" did not exist, but that was what was going on. That Edwards had teenage daughters who knew about some of the incidents certainly made him more sensitive to such issues.

Still, Edwards would probably not have reacted so strongly except for another factor: most of the young men were church members. These were not fourteen-year-old boys to be disciplined by their parents, but rather young men in their twenties. In the Northampton Covenant two years earlier, the young people, then at the height of their collective spirituality, had promised solemnly to "strictly avoid all freedoms and familiarities in company, so tending either to stir up or gratify a lust of lasciviousness." Yet even at that time some of the young men had already been sharing the books and joking about them, at least among themselves. For Edwards that was not the relatively trivial issue it might have been in itself because some of these same young men had been simultaneously partaking in monthly communion at the church. Scripture warned strongly against "eating and drinking judgment to yourselves" by partaking of the Lord's Supper unworthily. Edwards had repeatedly warned his congregation that those who partook in a hypocritical or unrepentant way of the bread and wine were like those at the crucifixion who had mocked Jesus. In fact, some of the young men had joked about the underground books as "the young folks' Bible."

Apparently driven by this combination of emotionally charged concerns, Edwards handled the situation badly. First, after a church service, he not only publicly announced the nature of the offense but also read a list of names of young men and women who were to meet with a committee to investigate the matter. In reading this list he failed to make a distinction between the accused and those who were merely witnesses. Some young people from leading families were in the latter group, so that by the time parishioners got home from church much of the town was "all on a blaze" about the matter. The investigation wore on for months as the townspeople divided on the matter. In one colorful confrontation, a number of the young people were waiting at the Edwards home to meet with a formidable church judicial committee that included Colonel John Stoddard, the chief magistrate and judge of the region. As time dragged on, Timothy Root, one of the principal offenders (and a communicant church member), asked if he could leave and come back. When told "no," Timothy announced loudly, "I won't worship a wig." He and his cousin Simeon then took off for the local tavern. He also declared (in a good example of how a Calvinistic low view of human nature might make one a revolutionary) that the committee members "are nothing but men molded up of a little dirt" and "I don't give a turd" and "I don't give a fart" for any of them. Insubordination was now added to the original accusations.

The ringleaders, the two Roots and one other, were finally censured. Edwards, however, lost more than they did. The pastor who had once found such success with his ministry among young people now appeared too brittle, a reactionary who made a mountain out of a molehill. He, in the meantime, experienced disappointment once again with how, once the revival fires had cooled, the town reverted to its usual pettiness, bickering, and lack of spirituality.

This otherwise minor little drama proved to be a psychological turning point in Edwards's relationship to his Northampton parishioners. Until now, despite recurrent squabbles, the townspeople had accepted Edwards well, often with enthusiasm. He had effectively led them to spiritual heights and guided them through dark valleys. The mid 1740s would prove, however, to be a particularly trying time. The town was tested by warfare and an unusual toll of illness and death. Edwards would struggle to bring them through these trials, but this time he would not be able to reignite the revival fires.

CHAPTER SEVEN

A World in Conflict

Some who theorize about religious revivals assume that they are products of social tensions and hence more likely to take place in times of rapid change or high stress. Northampton's experience runs contrary to such assumptions. The years from 1734 to 1742, when the most intense revivals took place, were not times of unusual social change or external conflict. The mid-1740s seem a more trying era for the town, yet it was then that awakenings diminished. Edwards, who watched such things closely, believed that other conflicts often distracted people from religious interests.

Wartime

The outbreak of war did the most to change the atmosphere in Northampton and to amplify other tensions. In the spring of 1744 (around the same time Northampton was in a dither about its young men), France joined Spain against Great Britain in the War of the Austrian Succession (1740-1748). Since New France was just north of New England, that brought what the new Englanders called "King George's War" much closer to home. Most immediately the French entry into the war meant a renewal of the threat of Indian attacks.

Colonel John Stoddard was the principal military commander for western Massachusetts, and he soon took charge of overseeing a new line of forts to the west that would at least inhibit raids on the Connecticut River Valley by Indians loyal to the French.

By winter and spring of 1745 Northampton was deeply involved in another dimension of the war — one of the earliest displays of what would become a characteristic pattern of an American mix of patriotism and piety in response to an international conflict. The French had a great fortress at Louisbourg on Cape Breton Island near Nova Scotia that threatened New England shipping and fisheries. When war broke out, the governor of Massachusetts came up with an audacious plan for New Englanders to sail a military force to Louisbourg to capture the fortress. People all over New England enthusiastically embraced the venture. From Northampton Major Seth Pomeroy raised a company of fifty men from the region to join the expedition. William Pepperell of Maine, a pious layman who happened to be an admirer of Edwards, was named commander-in-chief to lead New England's forces.

New England did not have a professional army or much military experience, yet as the most intensely Protestant region in the colonies they had the strongest suspicions of the Catholics to the north, and they had high hopes that they could bring down the French Catholic citadel. Drawing on its Puritan heritage, New England supported the campaign with concerted prayer and special days of fasting. Old Lights and New Lights temporarily laid aside their differences as they joined in what Edwards called "an extraordinary spirit of prayer," greater than any public event he had witnessed. Coincidentally, George Whitefield had returned to the region as the plans for the expedition were being laid. Resentments against some of his divisive comments remained strong, but Whitefield moderated his tone and helped unite the region in the war effort. He preached to the troops and furnished the army with a sort of crusaders' motto, *"Nil desperandum Christo duce"* (No need to fear with Christ as our leader). Northampton, like other towns, held fast days, and relatives of the soldiers met regularly to pray for the success of the troops.

Benjamin Franklin in Philadelphia, while wishing his fellow New Englanders well, was skeptical of whether their reliance on prayer would improve the prospects for the amateur army. Writing to his older brother John, he tried out a bit of satire that might have served for a "Silence Dogood" piece had the old *New England Courant* still been around. "Some seem to think forts are as easy taken as snuff," he scoffed. Alluding to the days of fasting and all the other daily prayers in New England households, he calculated that from February, when the expedition started, to when he was writing in May there would have been "forty-five million of prayers; which set against the prayers of a few priests in the garrison, to the Virgin Mary, give a vast balance in your favor." If the New Englanders lost, as Franklin clearly expected, "I fear I shall have but an indifferent opinion of Presbyterian prayers in such cases, as long as I live." He added a word of advice to the pious: "Indeed in attacking strong towns I should have more dependence on *works,* than on *faith.*"

Too bad Franklin's satire was not published, since then there might have been a classic rebuttal from Edwards when, as it turned out, the siege worked and the great fortress fell to the New Englanders. Edwards and other New England preachers viewed the many circumstances that led to the victory as just short of miraculous. Unusually good weather aided the launching of the expedition, and later weather delays only kept it from arriving before the ice melted. The French bungled things at crucial moments. Just when the English were about to give up weeks of siege and attempt a desperate assault against the walls (which due to a hidden trench were twice as high as they appeared), the French garrison surrendered. Edwards concluded that it all was "a dispensation of providence, the most remarkable in its kind, that has been in many ages, and a great evidence of God's being one that hears prayer."

National allegiances at this time still had major religious components, as they had since the Reformation. Europe long had been divided between Protestants and Catholics in an extended sort of "cold war" that periodically broke into open conflict. National allegiances were determined by the faith of the monarch, and nations might move from one church to the other as a result of a dynastic change or conquest. In England such contests had been particularly intense. As recently as 1685 to 1688, England's King James II of the House of Stuart had been Catholic. When a Protestant prince, William of Orange, invaded England and displaced James, Protestants hailed it as the "Glorious Revolution," especially because it ended the immediate threat of a full Catholic takeover. England united with Presbyterian Scotland in 1707 to form Great Britain, with the explicit provision that successive monarchs must be Protestant. When the first King George of the German House of Hanover (now Windsor) took over in 1714, New Englanders hailed them defenders of "the Protestant interest."

Not long after New Englanders were thanking God for their own glorious victory over the French at Louisbourg, the Roman Catholic threat to Great Britain itself dramatically reemerged. In the autumn of 1745, Charles Edward, the heir to the Catholic House of Stuart, landed in Scotland, proclaimed himself king, and moved an army into England. "Bonnie Prince Charles," as his Highland Scottish Catholic supporters called him, or "the Young Pretender," as he was known to Protestants, was not finally defeated until the bloody battle of Culloden in April 1746.

Edwards, who had a number of ministerial correspondents in Scotland, followed these events with keen interest and once again saw God's extraordinary work in the defeat of the Young Pretender. The Northampton pastor's loyalty to Great Britain had a paradoxical element. On the one hand, true to his Puritan heritage, he lamented that England was religiously lax and, despite some popular revivals, becoming worse all the time, especially in its morals and in the spread of liberal views of theology associated with the Enlightenment. On the other hand, he viewed international politics through an essentially Old Testament lens. From that viewpoint he saw Great Britain, the Hanoverian kings, and their armies as raised up by God to spread the Protestant cause. If Protestantism was to succeed in its missions to Indians in North America, for example, as Edwards fervently hoped and expected, then Catholic powers would have to be defeated to clear the way.

Edwards's political views about his homeland anticipated in some respects what would become a characteristic pattern in later American evangelicalism. Although such conservative Protestants long lamented the moral decline and depravity of their nation in its domestic policy, when it came to foreign policy they typically saw God as supporting the American cause. Often they viewed American expansion as a God-ordained opportunity for Christian missions. Edwards saw British foreign affairs through the Protestant/Catholic categories of his era. For later American Christians, other loyalties, such as to American political ideals, usually overshadowed and displaced explicitly ecclesiastical concerns in foreign policy. Protestant/Catholic political differences receded and eventually nearly disappeared, but for many Americans the overall pattern of seeing God's hand in American destiny and mission has remained.

The Coming Millennial Peace

Edwards framed his intense Protestant loyalties in an elaborate system of biblical and millennial interpretation that was more peculiar to his era. Edwards's view of history and of the end times was what today would be called "postmillennial," meaning a belief that Christ would return to earth only *after* a millennial golden age. (Most evangelical Protestants today are "premillennialists," meaning that they believe Jesus will return to earth *before* the millennial kingdom over which he will personally rule.) Edwards and many other postmillen-

nial interpreters of his day were just as biblicist as interpreters today, and they looked as carefully for literal interpretations of biblical prophecies, but they worked from premises shaped by the
Reformation conflict. Protestant interpreters typically assumed that
the "Antichrist" of the book of Revelation must be the Papacy. They
then made various calculations as to how long it would be before the
Antichrist would be destroyed, thereby clearing the way for the millennium. When Edwards read the newspapers he carefully looked
for anything that signaled a setback for Catholic powers, and he copied these into a notebook. Catholic defeats and the worldwide
spread of revivals were the chief things that must happen to prepare
for the millennial age, which Edwards thought might arrive around
the year 2000.

One fascinating feature of Edwards's millennialism is that he
was much more of an optimist than most people realize. Edwards
believed that the entire world would be evangelized in preparation
for the coming millennium. In that last golden age, lasting a literal
one thousand years, virtually everyone would become truly Christian, due to world awakenings. That meant that the vast majority of
people who ever lived would be eternally saved. Edwards (who, like
Benjamin Franklin, enjoyed counting things) was aware that the European population was beginning to expand in geometrical propor-
tions. Projecting that trend into the future, he calculated that well
over ninety percent of people in the world's history would live in the
centuries yet to come, and that the vast majority of them would be
saved. The population increases would also be enhanced by the end-
ing of warfare and reduction of disease that mass conversions would
entail. In a golden age when almost everyone was Christian, peace
and justice would reign and all would benefit from widespread social and moral reform.

So even as Edwards saw the awakening fade at home, he drew on
his more optimistic global perspective to sustain his enthusiasm for
promoting international revivals. Scotland had experienced great

awakenings similar to those in the colonies, and in 1747 Edwards published a book designed to promote a "concert of prayer" with awakeners in Scotland. He stated his entire thesis in his less-than-catchy title: *An Humble Attempt to Promote Explicit Agreement and Visible Union of God's People thro' the World, in Extraordinary Prayer, for the Revival of Religion, and the Advancement of Christ's Kingdom on Earth, Pursuant to Scripture Promise and Prophecies Concerning the Last Times.* In this work he explained that temporary setbacks and persecutions of the church were to be expected even though the progress of the work of God's Holy Spirit was inevitable. Defeats of the Roman Catholic Antichrist, as at Louisbourg or of the "Young Pretender" in Scotland, helped confirm God's hand in the overall pattern.

Mission to the Indians

Living as he did on the frontier of a Protestant empire with Catholic French and Indians to the immediate north and west, Edwards's intense Protestant/British loyalties were not simply abstract byproducts of theology. They were also momentous practical matters of life and death. The possibility of Indian raids was one of the things that defined life in the Connecticut River Valley. In 1704 Indians and their French officers had raided the town of Deerfield, Massachusetts, just fifteen miles north of Northampton, killing thirty-nine people and carrying more than a hundred individuals into captivity. New Englanders were horrified by the "Deerfield Massacre," and especially during periodic wartimes many lived in terror of another such episode. The Edwards and Stoddard families were especially scarred by these attacks; two of Edwards's young cousins and their mother, Edwards's aunt and a stepdaughter of Solomon Stoddard, died at the hands of the Indians. The father, the Rev. John Williams, and the remaining children were carried into captivity in Canada.

Eventually the surviving Williamses were "redeemed" from captivity and came home. However, one young daughter, Eunice, refused to come home, adopting Indian ways and, to the greater horror of her family, converting to Catholicism. For years all of New England prayed for her restoration, and these would have been among the family prayers that Jonathan grew up with. In 1740 Eunice and her Indian husband actually visited her brother, the Reverend Stephen Williams, in Longmeadow, Massachusetts. Edwards, a close friend of Stephen, came to preach for the occasion, but to no avail.

These excruciatingly painful family experiences with the Indians made the large Williams-Stoddard-Edwards clan particularly zealous to promote Indian missions. They recognized that the failure to keep friendship with the natives was one of New England's great shortcomings. After a promising beginning for missions to the Indians under John Eliot in the mid-1600s, King's Philip's War in 1675-76 — the most destructive per capita in American history — permanently alienated many of the Indians and hindered the success of Protestant mission efforts.

Colonel John Stoddard had a special interest in these efforts. As a young soldier, he had been staying at the Williamses' house when it was overrun by Indians during the Deerfield Massacre of 1704. He had barely escaped with his life. In later years he became not only a military leader in charge of defending against Indian attacks but also a chief negotiator in trying to keep peace with them. Stoddard advised the British, who were often inept in working with Indians, that they must deal honestly with the Indians if they were to keep their trust. In the later 1730s, shortly after the first awakening in Northampton and the Connecticut River Valley, Stoddard and a number of members of the extended Williams family helped organize a small mission town in Stockbridge, Massachusetts, in the mountains of the southwest corner of the colony.

Edwards, shaped by this family history and his hope for worldwide revival, was already deeply concerned for Indian missions when he was dramatically confronted by the personification of the cause in 1747. That spring David Brainerd, a gravely ill twenty-nine-year-old missionary to the Indians, came to the Edwards home to spend what would be the last months of his life. Brainerd had been one of the most ardent New Light students at Yale when Edwards spoke there in 1741 and had eventually been expelled for, among other things, his remark that one of the tutors "had no more grace than a chair." The young man had since proved his own deep spiritual dedication by undertaking on his own the most arduous missionary travels into the wilds of Pennsylvania, though he was rewarded with little success. Later he gained a better response while working in an Indian village in New Jersey, but his work was cut short by tuberculosis.

The juxtaposition of Brainerd's dedication to evangelizing the Indians and the situation in Northampton was dramatic. Since the previous summer, as King George's War continued, the town had been living with the constant tension of a possible Indian attack. The Edwards home had to be "forted in," and Jonathan wrote to his daughter Esther, who was visiting in Long Island during the summer of 1746, "Here we have been in much fear of an army suddenly rushing in upon the town in the night to destroy it." During these years, small bands of Indians had several times raided the neighboring village of Southampton and killed a few of its residents. Although Northampton escaped direct attack, it often felt like it was under siege, but by an unseen enemy.

When Brainerd arrived in May 1747, Sarah Edwards had only recently delivered their tenth child. The crowded household also included at least one other young New Light preacher, Eleazar Wheelock (later founder of an Indian school and Dartmouth College), who also had taken ill and was convalescing there. The care of Brainerd fell to the second eldest daughter, Jerusha, who had just turned seventeen. The friendship of Jerusha and Brainerd soon became a legendary and poignant love story.

Jonathan greatly admired, even loved, Brainerd for his intense spirituality, and Jerusha may have been especially ready to dedicate herself to his care for the same reason. She was probably the most deeply spiritual of the Edwards children. It happened that she had been named for a younger sister of Jonathan, who had also been renowned for her saintliness but had died in her late teens. The younger Jerusha's piety was forged by the same revival fires that shaped her mother's remarkable experience. When in June it was decided that Brainerd might benefit from a horseback ride to Boston, Jerusha went along to care for him. After they returned to Northampton, Brainerd's health steadily declined. Jerusha stayed at his side to attend him until his death in October. As he was dying, Brainerd told Jerusha, "If I thought I should not see you and be happy with you in another world, I could not bear to part with you. But we shall spend an happy eternity together."

The bittersweet sequel was that only four months later Jerusha suddenly fell ill of unrelated causes. She died within a week. Jonathan was especially devastated. To a correspondent in Scotland he confided that she was "generally esteemed the flower of the family." In Northampton the stricken father preached on a theme from the book of Job, "Youth is like a flower that is cut down." He rejoiced in her heavenly rewards but also used the occasion to challenge other young people to mend their ways. What if one of them was next? What if at the funeral the best a parent might say was, "This my departed child was an eminent frolicker, much of a gallant, a jolly companion"? The Edwardses, reassured by their saintly daughter's faith, buried her next to Brainerd, symbolizing their eternity together.

Edwards had already been so impressed by Brainerd's spiritual example that he had put aside what he considered a crucially important treatise on the freedom of the will in order to edit Brainerd's diaries. Jerusha had probably been helping him produce this *Life of David Brainerd.* In it Edwards was not so much interested in the

drama of Brainerd's arduous missionary trips as he was with the inner spiritual life of a saint who sacrificed everything for the kingdom of God.

The Life of David Brainerd eventually became the most popular of
Edwards's major works. During the nineteenth century many missionaries carried it with them on their journeys and were inspired by
the record of Brainerd's spiritual struggles and his dependence on
God. In the era before modern consumer culture, pious Americans
typically viewed the self as something to be controlled and sup-
pressed in service to God and to fellow humans. Eventually the alternative ideal that the self is to be celebrated and that self-fulfillment
is the chief end of life came to be the more prominent American
theme. Anticipations of that latter ideal were already present in Edwards's time, most famously represented in Benjamin Franklin's
Autobiography, essentially the story of a self-made man. Through
much of the nineteenth century, however, Edwards's Life of Brainerd
offered a model of the self-sacrificing person that competed with
Franklin's ideal as a classic American account of what it meant to be
truly fulfilled.

Conflict in Northampton

In Northampton Edwards was becoming increasingly uneasy about
having to deal with young men who aspired to personal independence rather than to obedient self-sacrifice on the Brainerd model.
Although in the later 1740s no one would have guessed that in
twenty years Massachusetts would be in the early stages of a major
political revolution, the generation of men who would lead that revolution was already coming on the scene in Edwards's time. Some of
the ideas and attitudes that would soon blossom into full-blown revolutionary ideology were also beginning to emerge. Particularly, the
next generation would question the tradition of strict control of the

society from the top down, such as Edwards and his patron John Stoddard took for granted in Northampton. Edwards would encounter the glimmer of these new ideals before the dawn of a new, revolutionary era.

One dimension of "the rights of men" as it was emerging in this male-dominated society was that it meant precisely the rights of *men,* and not incidentally their right to more sexual freedom. Benjamin Franklin, for instance, showed little regard for the institution of marriage. Edwards deeply opposed such trends. In his sermon on Jerusha's death, he contrasted her spirituality with some common practices of the young, such as "that shameful lascivious custom of handling women's breasts, and the different sexes lying in beds together." The latter referred to the New England custom of "bundling," in which parents allowed unmarried couples to spend the night together in bed, though fully clothed. Although that was supposed to be a "safe" alternative to sexual intercourse, it did not always turn out that way: even in Northampton, which was more conservative than were many other parts of New England, one in ten married couples had their first child within eight months of marriage. So long as such couples married, the church accepted confessions and lived with the realities.

Edwards was particularly insistent that the couples must marry, assuming the father could be identified. That was the issue in a particularly troubling case that emerged in 1747 involving one of his own younger cousins, Lieutenant Elisha Hawley. The young soldier was from one of the elite families in Northampton. He was the son of Edwards's well-to-do Uncle Joseph Hawley, who had committed suicide at the height of the first awakening in 1735. Elisha acknowledged that he had fathered twins (only one surviving) with Martha Root. The Roots were of a lower social class, and the two families agreed to a cash settlement rather than marriage. Edwards, however, insisted that the two should marry. It was not right, he reasoned, for a man to have his pleasure with a woman and then be able to buy his way out of long-term responsibility. The case dragged on for two years. Eventually a council of local ministers ruled against Edwards, saying that if Hawley confessed to his sin, then the financial settlement would be an acceptable alternative to an inappropriate marriage. Perhaps the most important consequence of this fracas was that Elisha's older brother, Joseph Hawley, Jr., an up-and-coming lawyer in the community, turned against his uncle. Edwards had apparently mentored Joseph Jr., who had attended Yale and had originally planned to enter the ministry. After having served as a chaplain during the war, Joseph Jr. came back with more liberal theological views. When the fight over marriage broke out, he took the side of his younger brother against his pastor and uncle.

An Ill-Timed Revolution

Such incidents would have amounted to nothing more than the inevitably bitter squabbles in a small town had Edwards not been planning his own sort of revolution. As we saw earlier, his grandfather Solomon Stoddard had long ago loosened the requirements for communicant church membership in Northampton. Basically Stoddard's standard had been that to be a full member, including participation in communion, or the Lord's Supper, a person had only to affirm Christian doctrine, assent to live as an obedient church member, and to live a life free from scandal. No claim to a conversion experience was required. When Stoddard had instituted such changes some seventy years before, they were a departure from earlier Puritan practice. Jonathan was probably always uneasy with the more open practice in Northampton, but for the time being he had learned to live with it.

Now he determined to reverse the longstanding Northampton policy. Like many other Christians, he took seriously the biblical warning about the Lord's Supper that "he that eateth and drinketh unworthily, eateth and drinketh damnation to himself, not discerning the Lord's body" (1 Corinthians 11:29). Edwards followed the Puritan tradition of interpreting this verse in terms of a covenant. The bread and the wine of the Lord's Supper symbolized the body and blood of Christ as a seal of the most solemn promises between Christ and believers. Those who partook lightly mocked those promises — and did so at their own peril. If, as the awakening underscored, conversion to heartfelt belief was so important, and if the Bible warned that the Lord's Supper was only for true believers, Edwards now felt the need to bring his church into line.

Unfortunately, his timing could hardly have been worse. He had somewhat obscurely intimated his changing views on church membership in *Religious Affections* in 1746, and had been trying out his proposed change privately among friends and visitors, but he had not revealed it to the townspeople. The church was in a bit of a doldrums during the war, and Edwards was waiting for a case in which someone would apply for communicant membership whom he was sure could meet the new higher standards. In the meantime, calamity intervened. In June of 1748 Colonel John Stoddard was in Boston consulting about military affairs and was struck down by a stroke. As the director of military operations on the western frontier, Stoddard had been under strain for some time. Although Massachusetts had a line of forts to help protect it, they were an exceedingly porous defense against Indian attacks. At one point he wrote, "I have as many messengers with evil tidings as Job had, though I have not so much patience." Stoddard had also been the leading organizer of a planned attack on Quebec — an endeavor that became a fixture in American wars — but it was never carried out. When Stoddard was felled by his stroke, it was Sarah Edwards (who may have been in Boston on her own) who cared for him. A few days later he died.

Stoddard's death created a momentous hole in the affairs of Northampton's leadership. In this hierarchical society Stoddard had overseen the town as its chief magistrate, judge, and military leader. He was also deeply pious, the most influential layperson in the church, and a close ally and patron of Edwards. For Edwards to effectively reverse Solomon Stoddard's standard for church membership, he would have first needed to gain the support of Solomon Stoddard's son, who was presumably loyal to his late revered father's ways.

Now suddenly it was too late to do that, but Edwards went ahead anyway. In December of 1748 a pious young man came forward for communicant church membership, and Edwards asked him to sign a statement that would amount to what he considered a "credible" profession of heartfelt faith. To many of the townspeople, this looked suspiciously as though Edwards had waited until John Stoddard was out of the way before attacking Solomon Stoddard's system. Soon people were up in arms, and the young man withdrew his application, not wanting to be the occasion for such an explosive controversy. Edwards continued to press ahead anyway, and in the spring he found a qualified young woman willing to become a full communicant under his terms.

When the lid blew off as the town erupted in an overheated controversy, Edwards was caught off guard. He had judged his reversal of Stoddard's position as a *moderate* reform. It seemed moderate if one was thinking, as he was, in terms of the larger issues of the day. The old Puritan heritage had long struggled with the tension between being a pure church made up only of certified believers or being a state church, embracing more or less the whole community. Seventeenth-century American Puritans had typically required an account of conversion, often including specified steps, for full communicant membership. Stoddard and his followers had gone in the opposite direction. Edwards wished something in between: new communicants would have to provide only a "credible profession" of heartfelt commitment, not an elaborate account of their conversions. This, he believed, was sufficient to protect the purity of the church while at the same time keeping membership open to all in the town who showed reasonable evidence of true conversion.

Edwards also wanted to retain one tax-supported church for the whole town rather than resort to separatism. In many New England towns, radical New Lights, insisting on a pure church of converts only, had withdrawn from the established church to form a new congregation. Such post-awakening zeal had torn apart many of the towns of the region. Furthermore, adding to the disruption, by this time quite a few of the New Light separatists had gone a step further and become Baptists. These radicals reasoned that infant baptism was a leftover of the old state-church system, in which it had been assumed that every child in the community would become at least a baptized church member. By contrast, they insisted that only adult baptism was consistent with the idea that the church should be made up of converts only. This Baptist movement, which had sprung out of the New England awakenings, would soon spread south and eventually become the largest type of Protestantism in the United States.

Edwards wanted to avoid separatism and certainly had no time for the Baptists, but he was proposing something that many townspeople saw as similarly divisive. They soon discovered that Edwards, in addition to raising the requirements for communicant church membership, was proposing to tighten the standards for the other sacrament, baptism. Most of New England, including Northampton, had for several generations practiced what was called the "halfway covenant." As we saw in chapter three, this meant that baptized children of the church who as adults did not become full communicant members would still be considered "halfway members" and so could have *their* children baptized. The promises of the covenant, according to Reformed teaching, extended from generation to generation, so New Englanders had adopted this practice which allowed almost everyone in the community to be baptized.

When Northamptonites found out that Edwards wanted to revoke the revered Solomon Stoddard's standards for admission to full communicant membership *and* forbid baptism of the children of halfway members, many were infuriated. In Northampton, as in most of Christendom, baptism into the Christian community had seemed a birthright. Now it was to be taken away so Edwards could create a purer church. What if one's own grandchildren were not to be baptized! Edwards later said that he believed he might have been able to convince the majority to reverse Stoddard's policies regarding admission to communicant membership (though he was probably too optimistic about that), but that it became clear that his parishioners would never have given in regarding his restrictions on baptism.

The Edwards family and the town suffered through an ugly year of controversy. Townspeople held countless official and unofficial meetings. The ringleader of the opposition to Edwards was his nephew Joseph Hawley Jr., the young lawyer. Many older members who venerated the memory of Solomon Stoddard also opposed Edwards. Even before Edwards had proposed his revolution, townspeople had been bickering with the pastor. Yearly town meetings where they set his salary had often been particularly petty. Edwards repeatedly pointed out that his salary never kept up with inflation and argued that he needed more for his ever-growing family. Northampton, Edwards believed, was especially prone to contention, and he had often preached about that. The war years had only made things worse. Northamptonites lived with anxiety about the possibility of Indian attack, but another, more often devastating enemy lurked within, as illness was rampant. Between 1745 and 1748 some 140 citizens had died, or about one in every seven. Now all the pent-up tensions and frustrations in the town broke out in the controversy between the townspeople once renowned for the intensity of their piety and their famous pastor.

Trusting in his intellectual prowess, Edwards believed that he could persuade most people by argument. He even published a treatise on the occasion. But minds were already made up. Finally, the matter was settled by calling in a council of clergy and laymen from ten surrounding churches. When the council polled church members, only twenty-three of the 230 men who voted supported Edwards. The visiting council was already divided along partisan lines, and on a close vote they agreed with the town majority to immediately dismiss Edwards from his pastorate.

During these final proceedings, Edwards retained a remarkable outward serenity, but he was deeply hurt, even embittered. In his farewell sermon preached eight days after the decision he formally said goodbye to the congregation that had once so passionately followed his lead. Like a once-brilliant marriage that later broke up, the intensity of the past relationship only accentuated the unhappiness of the parting. Edwards took the opportunity to once again warn those who had rejected him of his concern for the state of their eternal souls. He also suggested, not too subtly claiming final victory, that when they would meet again in the last judgment his adversaries might have something to answer for.

As it turned out, the contending parties would be meeting again all too often prior to the last judgment. Edwards and his large family had nowhere to go and had to remain in Northampton for another year while he looked for a new position. To make matters all the more awkward, when the church leaders were looking for someone to fill the pulpit, they would sometimes have to ask Edwards, always making it pointedly clear that they could not find anyone else.

Edwards's painful dismissal tells us some things about his personality and character. First, it reveals that Edwards was not the shrewdest judge of everyday human dynamics. His timing for attempting his revolution so soon after the death of John Stoddard was disastrous. He also seemed to believe that eventually he could bring the congregation around simply by force of argument. He seems to have misjudged the degree to which such things depend on many other factors. He apparently underestimated the degree to which most of the townspeople had a sense of ownership of the church and of the right of their children or grandchildren to be at least baptized members of it. While Edwards stood for the logic of his principles, he was attempting suddenly to reverse longstanding sensibilities. As he himself later recognized, he also did not take sufficiently into account the degree to which many of the townspeople viewed the great Solomon Stoddard almost as a deity — and that they accordingly regarded a defense of Stoddard's views as a matter of high religious duty.

This episode also highlights how much Edwards was driven by dedication to principle. However much his bickerings with some of the townspeople might have reduced the reserve of good will, if Edwards had not proposed a revolutionary revision of rules for church membership, his pastorate would almost certainly have continued indefinitely. He was taking a huge risk, and he knew it, even if he miscalculated on the timing. Nonetheless, once he was convinced that he was correct and had settled on his course, he was willing to suffer bitter and costly consequences for himself and his family, all for a matter of principle. Whether we judge such firm determination as for good or for ill, it is a consistent trait in Edwards's life. It shaped him as a pastor, evangelist, defender of the awakenings, and promoter of missions. It would be equally apparent in the next direction his life would take.

CHAPTER EIGHT

A Missionary, a Scholar, and a President

—◦/◦/◦—

We can only imagine the pain and anxiety for Edwards and his family as they suddenly faced a most uncertain future. The longer they remained in Northampton, the worse the situation became. Soon after Edwards was dismissed from the Northampton pulpit, still in mid-summer, the town voted to prevent the Edwardses from using the pastureland they were usually granted on a yearly basis. By the fall the church voted not to ask him to preach, even if no one else were available. Soon some of his few loyal followers in Northampton were urging him to start a separate congregation.

Edwards was exploring other possibilities. Some of his correspondents in Scotland asked him to pastor a church there. He declined on the basis that he was reluctant to move such a large family across the Atlantic, and he also suggested that his now-proven lack of administrative skills might disqualify him from another major pastoral position. He considered a couple of smaller charges in New England, but what interested him most was the little Indian mission town of Stockbridge in the mountains of the southwest corner of Massachusetts. He visited there for most of the winter and then accepted a call to pastor its small congregation of New England settlers and to be a missionary to the Indians.

Transitions

Much else had been going on in the Edwards family during these years of the church crisis and dismissal. His daughters had been attracting suitors for some time. Samuel Hopkins, Edwards's student and later biographer who stayed in the household in the early 1740s, may have already had his eye on the very spiritual young Jerusha, to whom he presented a Bible several years before her fated love affair with David Brainerd. We know that the eldest daughter, Sally, was writing to another young missionary to the Indians, Elihu Spencer, in the winter of 1748 just before Jerusha's sudden illness and death.

Perhaps the most interesting case, or at least the one we happen to know most about, is that of the third daughter, Esther, who was described as "of great beauty." In the fall of 1748, when Esther was sixteen, Joseph Emerson, a young Massachusetts pastor, met Edwards at the Yale commencement and traveled home with him by way of Northampton. There, as he reported in his diary, he met "the most agreeable family I was ever acquainted with," an estimate doubtless enhanced by the fact that he was hopelessly smitten by the comely Esther. He returned a month later to ask for her hand in marriage, but Esther gave him no encouragement. Later that spring he recorded his continuing distraction by these unrequited hopes and prayed that he might find peace.

From time to time the older girls lived in homes of family friends, usually ministers in other towns. Typically one of the children would accompany Jonathan on trips to Boston or New Haven. Esther developed a very close friendship in Boston with Sally Prince, the daughter of one of Jonathan's closest allies there, the Reverend Thomas Prince, founder of the revival magazine *Christian History.* Sarah Sr. also liked to travel between pregnancies, probably in connection with weaning the latest infant. When one such trip to Boston was prolonged due to Colonel John Stoddard's sudden illness and death, an exasperated Jonathan, while recognizing "the calls of providence with regard to Col. Stoddard," wrote that the two oldest girls had taken to bed with "the headache" and that "we have been without you almost as long as we know how to be."

At home, in addition to caring for their younger siblings, the older daughters would be engaged in other household industries. Probably they kept busy on the spinning wheel. At one point they manufactured fans. When paper was scarce, Jonathan used scraps from the fans for some of his many notebooks. One of Sarah's most frequent reminders was a quotation from Jesus regarding picking up the crumbs after the feeding of the five thousand, "that nothing be lost." Frugality was a strict household rule.

Household industry was probably often accompanied by music. Sarah loved to sing, and Jonathan had been active in introducing four-part harmony into congregational singing. Likely the girls also played some musical instruments. They were also from an early age well-trained, apparently mostly at home, in reading and writing.

The year 1750 was a time of momentous changes for the family and, despite the sorrow of rejection, it was punctuated by moments of joy. In the spring Sarah bore their eleventh child (ten surviving) and third son, Pierpont. The eldest daughter, Sally, was now twenty-one. Elihu Spencer was now out of the picture and in June, just before the council met concerning her father's dismissal, she married a local man, Elihu Parsons. In November her younger sister Mary, who had just turned sixteen in the spring, married Timothy Dwight Jr., of one of Northampton's leading families. The Dwights were among Edwards's few supporters, and the young couple, who remained in Northampton, long had an uneasy relationship to the church. Their son, Timothy Dwight III, eventually became president of Yale and one of the most influential promoters of the broadly Edwardsean heritage in America of the early nineteenth century.

A Frontier Mission in Time of War

Throughout 1750 the family grappled with the anxiety of not knowing where they might go; in 1751 they faced the anxiety of knowing that they would be going. Stockbridge was across the rugged mountains of western Massachusetts and must have seemed like the end of the world compared to Northampton. The little missionary village, strung out along the Housatonic River, was made up of some two hundred Indians and ten English (New Englander) families. The idea behind the founding of the town in the 1730s had been that Indians needed to be settled and civilized according to European standards if they were to be successfully evangelized. Under the original missionary, John Sergeant, a young Yale graduate, 125 Indians had been baptized, and forty-two of them had become communicant church members.

Colonel John Stoddard had been a leader in founding the mission, and many of the other founders were part of the powerful Williams family that was intermarried with the Stoddards and hence related to Edwards. The original town squire at Stockbridge was Ephraim Williams Sr., the younger brother of the influential Rev. William Williams of Hatfield (near Northampton). Ephraim Williams had a brilliant and charming daughter, Abigail, who was still in her teens when the family moved to Stockbridge in 1737. Soon John Sergeant, the missionary, was deeply in love with Abigail, and the two were married in 1739. Abigail had cosmopolitan tastes and built a home that was elegant for the time. It still stands in Stockbridge today. Then in 1749 John Sergeant developed a throat canker and soon died.

Most of the Williams clan, although predominantly New Lights, viewed their cousin Edwards with some suspicion, especially after he took his stand against Solomon Stoddard's principles of church membership. They thought him too strict, and he had some fallings out with some of the younger "gentlemen" of the extended family.

Abigail was at first wary of Jonathan when he was a candidate to fill her late husband's position, but after his extended visit to Stockbridge early in 1751 she was at least temporarily won over. She wrote to a friend that "He is learned, polite, and free in conversation, and more catholic [widely informed and broad minded] than I had supposed." Abigail's half-brother, Captain Ephraim Williams Jr., had a far more negative view. He considered Edwards "not sociable" and a "great bigot." The town's schoolteacher, Timothy Woodbridge, however, favored Edwards, as did the majority of the church members, and he received the call.

Edwards moved in the summer and oversaw the expansion of the original mission house on the plain near the Indians. The Edwards family, full of trepidation, finally moved in October. By January, however, Edwards could write to his elderly parents that "They like the place far better than they expected," and that "the Indians seem much pleased with my family especially my wife." Esther, now twenty, wrote enthusiastically about sledding down the long hills and being pulled back up by Indian boys. Jonathan Jr., the second boy, aged six when they arrived, soon had Indian playmates and became fluent in the Indian languages.

The Stockbridge Indians were Mahicans, part of a once larger tribe that had found an alliance with the English helpful for their protection. The supporters of the mission, including the Massachusetts government and some wealthy contributors from England, were especially eager to reach out to another group of Indians, the Mohawks of the powerful Six Nations of the Iroquois Confederacy, who were crucial to English interests in North America. In general the French, in part because they had far fewer settlers in the region looking for land, were correspondingly more successful in recruiting Indian allies than were the English. The Mohawks were one of the exceptions who worked with the English. The attraction for the Mohawks at Stockbridge was that it was to provide boarding schools for Mohawk children as well as serve for some as a winter residence.

During Edwards's first summer in Stockbridge, some of New England's leaders met with an assembly of Mohawk chiefs to discuss the matter. Edwards preached to the Indians, presenting the gospel in simple terms. What he said revealed his view of the Indians. Although he believed the Indians to be religiously deprived and hence culturally inferior, he did not see them as naturally or intrinsically inferior to Europeans. Alluding to the time during the Roman Empire when the ancestors of the English had been "barbarians" prior to the arrival of Christian missionaries, Edwards assured the Indians, "It was once with our forefathers as 'tis with you." They had been in great darkness, but then they received the light of the gospel. "We are no better than you in no respect," he continued, "only as God has made us to differ and has been pleased to give us more light. And now we are willing to give it to you." Edwards believed that any nation might include true believers who, however humble their circumstances, might be spiritually superior to the greatest men anywhere. He also expected that one day there would be notable Indian theologians. First, though, Mohawks needed to accept the simple rudiments of the gospel of God's love, and for that they needed God's revelation in the Bible. The French Catholics, said Edwards, kept Indians in the dark by withholding the Bible from them. Even many English failed to support missions because "they choose to keep you in the dark for the sake of making a gain of you."

In this last remark, Edwards pointed to the greatest obstacle to English missions to the Indians. The English had claimed the Indians' lands and were relentlessly settling them at the expense of the natives. Only a minority of the settlers were interested in missions for their own sake, and even among those that were, such as the English families in Stockbridge, good will toward Indians was often undercut by desires for land and making a living. As the families expanded they wanted new land for younger sons and often took advantage of the Indians in buying their lands. The Williams family, though principal supporters of the mission, were leading offenders in this respect. Edwards soon lost their confidence by taking the side of the Indians and insisting on honest dealings. To make matters worse, Abigail Williams Sergeant held effective control over the fledgling schools designed for the Mohawks. Edwards, who wanted to gain control himself, believed the Williamses were misusing the funds.

Edwards hoped to manage the Stockbridge situation by inviting his friend and admirer, Brigadier General Joseph Dwight of Brookfield, Massachusetts, to settle in Stockbridge. Dwight, a wealthy merchant who had gained his military rank at Louisbourg, had supported Edwards in the communion controversy, and he had been a negotiator with the Mohawks. Edwards believed he would play the roles of the faithful aristocrat, magistrate, and patron, much as John Stoddard had done in Northampton. Dwight accepted, but soon it became apparent that Edwards had miscalculated on one point. Almost immediately after arriving in Stockbridge, Dwight fell under the spell of the charming and intelligent Abigail Williams Sergeant. By February 1752 the two were engaged to be married, much to Edwards's chagrin.

Edwards was convinced that the Williams family, led by Abigail, was mismanaging the boarding schools to serve their own interests. A lengthy controversy ensued. Dwight and the Williamses claimed that Edwards was the problem. However, after two years of letters, complaints, negotiations, and even the mysterious burning of a school building, the overseers of the mission, including officials of the Massachusetts government and British donors, finally ruled that Edwards was in the right and gave him control of the schools. By that time, it was almost too late. Most of the Mohawks who had been spending winters in Stockbridge had left in disgust. Though Edwards still had a parish church of Mahican Indians and English families, the boarding school was reduced to one Mohawk and five Mahican children.

Meanwhile other tensions disrupted village life. In the spring of

1753, a couple of English settlers in the region shot and killed the son of the leading Stockbridge Mahican. An English court eventually acquitted one man and convicted the other only of manslaughter. Many of the Stockbridge Mahicans were enraged, and it was even rumored that a few younger Mahicans were plotting with Iroquois to murder English colonists in the town. As often happened in American Indian missions, aggressive behavior by Euro-American settlers undermined already imperfect efforts of the missionaries themselves.

Elsewhere conflicts with Indians became so widespread that Benjamin Franklin organized the first inter-colonial American conference at Albany in upstate New York, only some thirty miles northwest of Stockbridge. Representatives of a number of the colonies met in the summer of 1754 to see if they could cooperate more effectively in response to increasing threats of Indians and their French allies. By that time hostilities had broken out farther south and west in what would become the French and Indian War. The delegates to the Albany Conference heard that the French had gained complete control of the Ohio Valley after taking over Fort Necessity from a force of Virginians led by a young colonel named George Washington.

Residents of Stockbridge and the other vulnerable villages of the Berkshire Mountains in far western Massachusetts were becoming intensely afraid of being overrun by Indians. In the late summer of 1754 a couple of Canadian Indians killed some local settlers and sent the whole region into a panic. Stockbridge became an armed camp, and the Edwards home had to be fortified. Despite pleas for more help, Stockbridge was a small outlying village and would never have enough protection to be able to ward off any sizeable attack.

Edwards's commitment to the mission was not dampened by the danger it now presented for him and his family. Edwards saw the Brainerd model of self-sacrifice as an example of what he believed should be the ideal for all Christians. Like the saintly young missionary, they should put love to God over love to everything else, including even family and their own comfort and safety. While at Stockbridge, Edwards developed this same point as a more universal philosophical principle. One of the greatest treatises that he wrote in the relative isolation of the mission village was called *The Nature of True Virtue.* In it he argued that the standards for virtue as derived from natural reason, as by the Enlightenment philosophers of his time, defined virtue too narrowly. Through the ages philosophers had praised virtues such as love for family, love for community, and love for nation. These might be good traits so far as they go, said Edwards, but they are part of true virtue only if they begin with love for God. All loves whose highest object is something less than God are partial loves rather than universal. Only if one starts with love to God and then sets one's sights on loving all that God loves can one participate in truly universal love. If one's object is to love all that God loves, then one can begin to achieve true self-sacrifice.

Edwards illustrated the principle of sacrificing all to serve God not only by remaining in Stockbridge but also by sending his second son, Jonathan Edwards Jr., to accompany a missionary into the wilds of the upper Susquehanna Valley. It was the spring of 1755, when all-out war was imminent. Gideon Hawley, the young missionary, had come to Stockbridge as Edwards's candidate to run the mission school but had become disillusioned after the conflicts over the mission. It didn't help that his school building was mysteriously burned with his possessions in it. The only effective way to reach the vitally important Mohawks, he decided, was to go to their own villages. Since ten-year-old Jonathan Jr. already had a good start in the Indian languages from his playmates, the Edwardses packed him off on a very dangerous venture in hopes of solidifying his language skills for later missionary work.

A letter that Jonathan Sr. sent to his young son is revealing of the father's priorities and temperament. After saying that he often thought of and prayed for Jonathan Jr., he reminded him to always keep God first in his sight, since only in God is true happiness. Then the father reported the death of an Indian playmate and said that this news "is a loud call of God to you to prepare for death." After expounding on this point, he sent the love of the family and the aged grandparents, whom he had seen in East Windsor, and signed it "Your tender and affectionate father."

What is especially striking about this letter is that we know that on the trip to East Windsor Edwards had a very dangerous fall from his horse, who had rolled completely over him. Yet he did not mention this bit of news to his ten-year-old, even as an admonition to caution. The father's focus was entirely on the spiritual well-being of his boy. As in his sermons, which never included personal illustrations, nothing about himself was to distract from the message that was crucial for eternity.

Not everyone in the family was so tranquil about putting God's will above all else regardless of dangers. We get the best sense of the personal dimensions of the situation from Esther, the second-oldest surviving daughter, whose story is fascinating in itself. In the spring of 1753 the Reverend Aaron Burr, the president of The College of New Jersey (which became Princeton) and a great admirer of Edwards, visited the family in Stockbridge. Burr, who was thirty-six, had come to ask for the hand of Esther, who was only twenty and whom he had only seen six years earlier. She quickly consented, and Sarah traveled with her to New Jersey for the wedding that same summer. The Edwardses' oldest son, Timothy, aged fourteen, also went along to enroll in the college.

Esther had a dear friend in Boston, Sally Prince, and the two resolved to keep up their friendship by sending each other extensive records of their thoughts and activities. They modeled their correspondence in part on the series-of-letters form of some of the newly invented novels, such as Samuel Richardson's *Pamela,* which were among the subjects they discussed. In Esther's account we occasionally get some glimpse of Edwards and his family. In one case, for instance, Aaron Burr is in Boston and Esther writes to Sally: "I imagine now this eve Mr. Burr is at your house. *Father* is there and some others. You all set in the Middleroom, *Father* has the *talk,* and Mr. Burr has the *Laugh,* Mr. Prince gets room to stick in a word once in a while. The rest of you set and see, and hear, and make observations to yourselves . . . and when you get up stairs you tell what you think, and I wish I was there too."

Esther soon had two children and in the fall of 1756 made the arduous journey to Stockbridge, in part to show off her six-month-old son, Aaron Burr Jr. (later the Vice President of the United States who shot Alexander Hamilton), to his grandparents. The French and Indian War was at its height and not going particularly well for the British. General Braddock's defeat and death in western Pennsylvania in July 1755 had caused consternation throughout the colonies. In September that year Stockbridge was rocked at the news of the death of Colonel Ephraim Williams Jr. (Edwards's antagonist) in a deadly ambush in the Battle of Lake George to their north. Also killed was one of the most important Indian friends of the English and of the Stockbridge project, the Mohawk leader Hendrick, with whom Edwards had worked closely and whom he greatly admired.

The next fall, around the time of Esther's visit, the French general Montcalm was finding success in the region north and west of Stockbridge. Esther was "scared out of my wits about the enemy." After the second day of her stay there was an alarm, so that most of the Indians moved into the fortified Edwards house and grounds. Knowing that she ought to submit to God's will, the young mother wrote, "I want to be made willing to die in any way God pleases, but I am not willing to be butchered by a barbarous enemy nor can't make myself willing." Finally, near the end of her stay she had a long open talk with her father, who "removed some distressing doubts that discouraged me much in my Christian warfare." She added, "what a mercy that I have such a Father! Such a guide!" Esther returned to the relative safety of Princeton while her parents trusted themselves and their younger children to God's hands amid the dangers of the unprotected wilderness. As they rejected pleas to move away from the war zone, Edwards wrote to a friend, "What will become of us, God only knows."

Answering Enlightenment Challenges

In the meantime Jonathan prayed to be preserved so that he could engage in another kind of "Christian warfare." Even before he had set off in his consuming careers as pastor, evangelist, apologist for the awakenings, and missionary, he had aspired to make some great contributions as a theologian-philosopher for the church of the ages. His dream seems to have been that he might be to the modern world something like the great early theologian Augustine (354-430) had been to the late Roman world. Since his youth he had been keeping great notebooks, sewing in new pages as needed, in which he drafted observations and arguments on almost the entire range of theological and biblical issues of the day. One advantage of living in Stockbridge was that because of its isolation and the relative smallness of his congregation, he had more time to write what he hoped would be a large series of major treatises. While he never got to some of his largest projects, his production in Stockbridge was remarkable.

The first order of intellectual business for the modern church, Edwards believed, was to combat the so-called "enlightened" philosophies of the day. In his view, these prevailing ideas were threatening the very basis of the traditional Christian faith. Many observers since then have agreed. For Edwards, as a Calvinist, the prevailing modern thought of his time presented a stark contrast to what should be central for finding what is true and good. Rather than starting with God and his revelation, "enlightened" philosophers typically started with human reason looking for natural laws. Calvinists, while valuing reason in its place, insisted that true understanding must start from recognizing human inadequacy and hence the necessity of depending on God alone. The spirit of the new age was to assert that humans were by nature essentially good and that they could find truth and virtue if only they freely chose to follow reason and their built-in moral instincts. Rather than allowing their reason and moral judgments to be guided by the truths revealed in Scripture, they were judging Scripture by how well it conformed to natural reason and moral sentiments.

Edwards believed that one of the most "pernicious" ideas in "this happy age of light and liberty" was the way its philosophers understood the "freedom of the will." Edwards's alertness to this issue grew out of his Calvinist heritage. Calvinists taught that the human will, like everything else, was ultimately subordinate to God's sovereignty, and that people in their fallen natural condition (that is without the change of heart that comes through regeneration) could not choose the truly good, since their choices would always be tinged with sinful self-interest. Enlightenment critics ridiculed this doctrine on the basis that people could not be held responsible for something they could not do. That seemed a matter of self-evident "common sense," as the popular philosophy of the day put it.

Careful philosopher that he was, Edwards focused his treatise *Freedom of the Will* on this "prevailing notion" that pure freedom of choice was essential to moral agency to which we might assign praise or blame. He blasted at this keystone of Enlightenment thought by pointing out that in ordinary life people's actions are constrained by their moral characters. In many of their choices, they are not truly free to act against their own deeply established character. For example, he said, suppose that an exceptionally virtuous woman was propositioned sexually by a scoundrel. Her own good character would make it inevitable that she would reject the proposition. Yet we do not say that she is less praiseworthy because her choice is so determined.

True freedom of the will, said Edwards, can mean only that we are free to choose what we *want* to do. There is no independent agent in us of "the free will" with which we make our choices independently of the constraints of our whole person. Rather, what we want or will to do is determined by our whole character, or previous choices, habits, commitments, dispositions, and appetites. Such personal characteristics that determine our choices do not make them any less "free," any less our own, or make us any less responsible for them. Edwards's treatise, which became a classic, has been much debated, especially in America for the century that followed, and by some philosophers even today.

Edwards's second major treatise written in Stockbridge defended the increasingly unfashionable Calvinist doctrine of "original sin." According to that teaching, everyone inherited from Adam and Eve both the guilt of the sin that brought the "Fall" of the human race and a fallen nature that made it inevitable that they would be sinners themselves. Edwards's argument on this topic was more theological, arguing that however difficult these doctrines might seem, they were taught in Scripture. Further, they were not out of accord with other common human experiences, such as that nations were sometimes punished as a whole for the acts of their leaders, or that children often suffered from the consequences of their parents' or ancestors' acts.

While at Stockbridge Edwards completed two other major works, *The Nature of True Virtue,* which we have already encountered, and its companion piece, *The End for Which God Created the World.* Edwards instructed that these be published in one volume. Edwards made his case in *True Virtue* on purely philosophical grounds; it was his only work in which he did not quote Scripture. So it was consistent with his central argument — that true virtue must begin with love to God — to pair this treatise with the other that provided its essential theological context.

The End for Which God Created the World addressed the question implied in its title: Why would a perfect being, such as God, need to create any less perfect beings? The answer, said Edwards, is that God is perfectly loving and so wishes to share that love with creatures capable of love. Edwards's starting point was that a loving God stands at the heart of the universe. So for Edwards the universe is most essentially personal; it is the creative expression of a person. Edwards's emphasis on personality at the center of reality presents a sharp contrast to most modern views. Since the Enlightenment many modern thinkers have built their theories on the premise that the universe is essentially impersonal, controlled by natural laws. Edwards challenged that view with a vital alternative: that at the core of reality is a loving God, and that love is the dynamic behind the creation of the universe and everything in it.

Starting with a sense of God's love at the center of reality then shapes the way we think of true virtue. At the core of reality is the beauty of the love of God pouring forth, so that the highest good is to return that love to God. If we truly love God, then we should also love what God loves, which is everything in creation, excepting evil or the negation of love. Modern philosophies, said Edwards, typically start in the wrong place, with humans and their needs. They see human happiness as the end of creation and then judge God by their limited standards. Each person, community, or nation has its own ideas of what will bring them happiness, and so people conflict with each other because their standards for virtue are too limited. Only true virtue, starting with love to the Creator of us all, can bring people together. Edwards called this universal love for others that should grow out of true love to God "love to being in general." His disciple, Samuel Hopkins, turned it into the more practical phrase "disinterested benevolence," meaning that one should act lovingly toward others with no regard for one's own interests. Hopkins's maxim of "disinterested benevolence" was influential in some early American reform movements, most notably antislavery.

Edwards had much more planned, and his situation in Stockbridge left him little to do but to work on his treatises. The war had rendered the mission school for the Mohawks impractical, and many of the Mahican men were off serving the English war effort. (A number of Stockbridge Mahicans served with Rogers' Rangers, a force immortalized in James Fenimore Cooper's novel, *The Last of the Mohicans,* set in the French and Indian War in 1757 and about a fictionalized tribe with a similar name.) The fact that Stockbridge was poorly defended rightly raised anxieties, but it was also isolated enough to be of little strategic value.

By this time, however, Edwards's life was becoming closely tied to that of his daughter Esther Edwards Burr. The College of New Jersey had recently moved to Princeton, and in the spring of 1757 it enjoyed a remarkable student revival fostered by its president, Aaron Burr Sr. Then in September, catastrophe struck. Aaron Burr Sr., only forty-one years old, suddenly took ill and died a few days later. The devastated trustees almost immediately turned to the obvious solution: Esther's father.

When Jonathan got Princeton's invitation, he was deeply torn. In a long letter to the trustees he offered two reasons why he hesitated to accept. First, he noted that he was prone to lengthy illnesses and an accompanying "low tide of spirits," which made him reluctant to give up his reclusive life in Stockbridge for the busy schedule and many personal dealings of a college president.

Second, he described in some detail two great works that he hoped to write. The most important would be what he called *A History of the Work of Redemption.* This would be a comprehensive treatise of all theology, put in a historical framework, detailing how God was bringing redemption throughout human history, centering in the coming of Christ and culminating in Christ's second coming. He had already preached a series of sermons of the same title on the historical developments, but now he planned a vastly more ambitious project of building on that framework "a body of divinity in an entire new method."

The other great work he was planning was to be a massive biblical study called *The Harmony of the Old and New Testament.* Edwards studied the Bible at length every working day, and for decades he had been developing large notebooks of these studies. He intended to assemble this material in an encyclopedic work that would tie all of Scripture together. Particularly he would emphasize the ways in which the New Testament revelation of salvation in Christ fulfilled numerous Old Testament prophecies and typologies.

An Interrupted Life

Despite his dedication to these projects and to the hope of rebuilding the Indian mission, Edwards felt he had to remain open to what could be a new call from God. The new college at Princeton was crucial to the New Light cause. Neither the more liberal Harvard nor his alma mater Yale was friendly to promoting ongoing awakenings. Edwards asked for a council of local clergy to give him advice. When they announced their decision that he should go to Princeton, he accepted it, though in tears. He set off almost immediately in January 1758, leaving his family to move later in the spring.

In Princeton Edwards moved in with Esther and his two young grandchildren, Sally and Aaron Jr., in the attractive president's home (still standing near the original Nassau Hall on Princeton's campus). He preached a few times in the college chapel, set a few lessons for students, and was officially installed as president in mid-February. That was all. Smallpox was spreading through the colonies. Inoculations against the disease had well-known risks and were controversial, but were also proven to improve chances of survival. Edwards, who always kept abreast of the latest scientific developments, had the whole family inoculated in late February. While Esther and the grandchildren came through fine, he soon contracted a secondary infection that eventually made it impossible for him to eat. He died on March 22, aged fifty-four.

Almost all his life he had been preparing for this moment. He had often preached to others about how they should be ready for death and righteous judgment at any minute, and he had disciplined himself with a regimen of devotion so that he would be prepared. In the weeks when he was wasting away he must have wondered why God would take him when he had so much to do. But submission to the mysteries of God's love beyond human understanding was at the heart of his theology. When he knew the end was near, he dictated a message to be sent to Sarah in Stockbridge, to "give my kindest love to my dear wife, and tell her, that the uncommon union, which has so long subsisted between us, has been of such a nature, as I trust is spiritual, and there fore will continue forever."

The family troubles, sadly, were far from over. Only two weeks after her father's death, Esther contracted an apparently unrelated fever and died a few days later. She was only twenty-six. In Stockbridge, Sarah Edwards was ill herself when she received these successive and almost unbearable blows. By September she was ready to travel and came to collect the orphaned grandchildren and take over the family affairs. Soon she contracted another illness and died on October 2, 1758. For thirty years, the family had seemed remarkably stable, enduring only one death, that of Jerusha. In less than one year it was irretrievably torn apart.

For us, it is fascinating to speculate on how American history might have been different had Jonathan Edwards remained at Princeton through the American Revolution. What if he had lived as long as his contemporary, Benjamin Franklin, who did not die until 1790? Edwards's most prominent successor at Princeton, the Reverend John Witherspoon, a Scottish philosopher, became the only clergyman to sign the Declaration of Independence. Witherspoon had taught James Madison, and Princeton was the site of a crucial battle in the war. Edwards's grandson, the orphaned Aaron Burr Jr., also studied at Princeton, and he rose to prominence in the revolution. He became a famous politician known for his family heritage, but not for his faith.

Even though Edwards usually deplored any rebellion against authority, he likely would have supported the revolution, as most of his friends and relatives did, believing that Great Britain had forfeited its authority. At the same time, Edwards put such a high priority on spiritual and theological matters that he would have been unhappy when his school and its supporters became so distracted by politics. Perhaps it is fitting that he lived through the Great Awakening but missed the American Revolution. History remembers the revolution as more significant than the awakening. Edwards would have disagreed.

What Should We Learn from Edwards?

─◦◦◦─

Many Americans are fascinated by the nation's founding, but not very many realize that there were two revolutions in the eighteenth-century British colonies. Before the political revolution of 1776 there was the religious revolution later known as the Great Awakening. Numerous American colonists rejected the staid routines of their established churches and responded to a message that appealed to them directly. This revolution revitalized the Protestant principle that salvation did not come through the authority of the church but rather directly through Christ's saving work to each individual. Redeemed believers might challenge, if necessary, church authorities who did not preach the personal message that one's heart must be radically changed for salvation. The result of this spiritual revolution was that the most vigorous of American churches were built on a popular voluntary principle, rather than on state control or inherited authority. During the generations following the American Revolution when the United States was still overwhelmingly Protestant, popular voluntary churches such as Methodists and Baptists were the ones that flourished most and set the tone for much of later American Christianity.

Conclusion

Understanding America's Paradoxical Heritage

If we forget about this spiritual revolution growing out of the Great Awakening and concentrate only on the nation's political origins, we have no way to explain one of the most striking features of contemporary America. The United States is one of the most industrialized, technologically advanced modern nations, and in many respects exceedingly secular; yet it is also remarkably religious. In contrast to Great Britain or western Europe, where churches are dwindling, in America the great majority of people profess religious faith. Probably the percentage who regularly attend churches is higher today than in the colonial era. Purely political and secular explanations of America's origins cannot explain this essential paradox of the nation that is simultaneously so secular and so religious.

Jonathan Edwards is a towering figure among the founding fathers of the first American revolution, the spiritual revolution of the awakening. He was the Thomas Jefferson of that revolution, not only its leading philosopher but also a sometimes controversial practical leader. George Whitefield was the George Washington of the awakening, the widely admired general in the field. Though such analogies are not exact, Edwards was certainly one of the major founders of the evangelical movement that became and remains the largest homegrown religious tradition in America. "Evangelicalism" is simply the collective term for all sorts of Christians who still emphasize the authority of the Bible, the importance of heartfelt conversion, and the urgency of evangelism and missions.

Evangelicalism is sometimes characterized as anti-intellectual, but the presence of Edwards in the heritage demonstrates that it also has a very different side. Edwards both promoted the revolutionary awakenings that fostered evangelicalism and tried to keep their popular appeals from undermining its theology. As the awakenings later swept through the early American republic, Edwards would not have been happy to see it fragment into so many popularized sub-types. Simplified messages inevitably had wider appeal than the more substantial theologies of the older Reformed traditions. Even so, Edwards continued to be revered among those branches of evangelicalism that remained Reformed, especially those with a New England heritage. Today evangelicalism is a huge coalition that includes many varieties, and while its most conspicuous sorts still are popular movements whose strengths are found elsewhere than in theological depth, these should not be mistaken for the whole. The evangelical movement also includes significant elements that preserve an Edwards-like combination of passionate faith and rigorous intellect.

Knowing the story of Jonathan Edwards also helps provide an answer to the much-debated question of the extent to which the United States had Christian origins. Edwards may be seen as representing the culmination of American Puritanism, the most formidable religious heritage in colonial America. His presence and that of his followers and other awakeners on the eve of the American Revolution certainly points to a significant Christian presence in eighteenth-century colonial America. Nonetheless, that observation needs to be balanced by the fact that ardently revivalist Christians of the revolutionary era were never close to being a majority. They did not think that the new nation or its immediate colonial predecessors were nearly Christian enough — that was why they believed there was such an urgent need for awakenings. They considered their era, despite its many public expressions of Christianity, to be unusually profane and far too influenced by sub-Christian philosophies growing out of the Enlightenment. Even though most of them endorsed the break with Great Britain because they thought the mother country was even more corrupt, the ardent revivalist Christians of the revolutionary era considered themselves to be a beleaguered minority in a nation that was far from being truly Christian.

Conclusion

Deepening Theological Insights

Even though Edwards played such a large practical role in helping to establish America's long-lasting revivalist tradition, he is best remembered and studied today for his profound theological insights. He developed his theology within his own Reformed or Calvinist tradition, and many of his particular insights are most celebrated by people of that heritage. Nonetheless, he was also exploring some of the highest reaches of the broader Christian heritage that transcend any one outlook. In these larger concerns that all Christians share, people of many traditions have been influenced by his observations.

The core principle that many religious believers might take from Edwards is that, if there is a creator God, then the most essential relationships in the universe are personal. Edwards started every inquiry with reference to God. If we want to understand the universe, then we must understand why God would have created it. As he argued in his treatise on *The End for which God Created the World,* the perfectly loving God of the Trinity must create in order to share that love with other morally responsible beings. The universe is, in other words, the result of the ever-expanding "big bang" (to use a later term) of God's love. If we see reality in its true dimensions, then, we see it as an ongoing expression of the beauty of love flowing from the Creator. If we sense the beauty of the light coming through the trees or the flowers in the fields, we are capturing small glimpses of the beauty of God's love. The physical world is the language of God; "the heavens declare the glory of God," as it says in the Psalms. Sin has partially corrupted the universe and often blinds humans from seeing its true essence. Yet for those who, through the work of the Holy Spirit, have their sight restored, they can see all of reality not as essentially impersonal but as, in its essence, a beautiful expression of God's love.

The most important relationship in this personal universe is to God the Creator and Redeemer. Edwards expressed the implications of this point best in his early revival sermon "The Divine and Supernatural Light," which is the best place to find a brief statement of his outlook. The Holy Spirit works in sinners so that, rather than being blinded to higher things by their love of self and fleeting pleasures, they see the beauty of the light of God's love. They are given "eyes to see" and are transformed or regenerated — "born again." This transformation is not merely a change in understanding, but also a change in one's affections, or in what one values and loves. One has a sort of "new sense" of God's glory, beauty, and love, and that exhilarating sensibility reshapes the priorities of what else one loves. Spiritually transformed people respond to God's love by loving first of all what God loves, or all that is good. In other words, the transformation of one's most essential personal relationship revolutionizes how one relates to the rest of reality.

Such a grand vision of a God-centered personal universe provides a sharp contrast to the essentially impersonal and materialistic view of the universe that has predominated since the Enlightenment of Edwards's day. Edwards was in fact directly countering the secularizing aspects of the Enlightenment trends that he saw around him. At the apex of the intellectual fashion of his day was deism, the sort of belief that many American founders such as Benjamin Franklin or Thomas Jefferson held. Impressed by the natural laws of physical reality in the Newtonian universe, deists thought of the universe as essentially a magnificently intricate machine governed by these impersonal laws. In order to account for the origins of the universe they believed there had to be a God who was like the cosmic watchmaker, who created a wonderful machine and let it run on its own without interference. They also believed that there must be moral principles built into the nature of reality, discoverable by natural reason. Essentially what the deists did was to distance God from creation. Though God might guide things through a general "Providence," the deity did not have to intervene with revelations or miracles, let alone through the Incarnation of his

Son, Jesus Christ. Truths about reality depended not on persons, but on abstract laws that could be discovered by impersonal rational processes.

Edwards, who was also impressed by the Newtonian understanding of physical reality, moved in just the opposite direction. Rather than viewing the physical world as essentially impersonal, he saw it, even in its scientifically predictable laws, as an ongoing and intimate expression of God's love. Through God's revelation of the redemptive work of Christ, fully disclosed only in Scripture, one could find the clues necessary for understanding a universe with personal love at its center. Everything, when rightly understood, pointed to God's redemptive love.

The impersonal view of the universe has dominated most of modern thinking. In modern civilization since the Enlightenment we have developed immense skills for controlling aspects of our immediate physical environment. While almost everyone appreciates these ways of increasing human comforts, this preoccupation with controlling the material world has encouraged a widespread materialist view of reality. We tend to value people on the basis of their material possessions, power, or physical appearance. We tend to think of the "real" world in terms of material forces and try to explain everything in such terms. Modern technology has built a technological civilization, where people gain power and influence by manipulating material things. These material things may indeed often be used to enhance human relationships, create virtual realities, or even to celebrate immaterial or spiritual things. Nonetheless, controlling material things is the practical source of power, the key to human advancement.

Benjamin Franklin was the great American prophet of this materialist and practical approach to reality. Franklin was renowned for his scientific experiments in electricity. He was a genius at applying practical principles, on a scientific model, to physical inventions and designing new social organizations. Franklin is an especially attractive example of this outlook because he dedicated numerous such practical inventions to the benefit of society. Many of the most impressive American achievements build on the foundations that Franklin helped lay.

This Franklinesque technical mastery, as attractive as it is, comes at a price. Our civilization tends to be dazzled by its own achievements, which are largely in improving prospects for material comforts and pleasures. But the more we are preoccupied with such matters, the more difficult it is to integrate spiritual sensibilities with our practical outlooks and attitudes. Even many religious believers tend simply to add God and a spiritual dimension to a largely materialistic view of things. Spirituality is likely to be regarded as a supplementary personal option, available for times of crisis. Less often does it substantially change how people live, or what they value. The United States, which is by far the most professedly religious of large industrialized nations, is also one of the most materialistic, hedonistic, and profane.

The Edwardsean alternative provides a basis for deepening the theological dimensions of many of the religious heritages that nonetheless thrive in the contemporary world. Edwards challenged the modern enlightened standards of his own day. He did so by insisting on starting with God as revealed in Scripture and in the redemptive work of Christ, rather than starting with currently popular standards of how humans might solve their own problems. Faith in God, then, was not something that was added on to the cultural norms of the day, but rather the beginning point, the lens through which all else was to be analyzed.

Edwards's theological vision was, moreover, not just a theoretical starting point, but based on the most intense sort of practical passion. Edwards's theology was practical because he always thought of God not as an abstract principle but as personally and intimately involved with all of creation. The God of the Scriptures, Edwards insisted, actively maintains an intimate relationship with the whole universe. Most importantly, this active God is doing his re-demptive work in Christ, who is at the very center of human history.

"Beauty" is the term that Edwards most typically used to describe the character of God's ongoing actions in creation and redemption. "Beauty" for Edwards is not just an object of passive contemplation, but rather a transforming power. If one sees a beautiful person, said Edwards, one cannot help but be drawn to that person. One's heart is drawn to that beauty, and one's actions will follow one's heart. So it is with the surpassing beauty of God as revealed in Christ. The most beautiful thing in all reality is for a perfectly good being to lovingly sacrifice himself for rebellious, undeserving, and ungrateful crea-tures. If one glimpses the perfect beauty of such love, one cannot help but be drawn to it. So the role of the evangelist is to convey the truth of God's revelation so that sinners who are blinded to true beauty by their self-love may, through God's grace, have their eyes opened to truly see it. If they do, their hearts will be changed and their lives will be dedicated to loving and serving God and others.

God-centered Integrity

Maybe the best way to sum up Edwards's character is to say that he had God-centered integrity. Having integrity suggests not only hon-esty, firmness of principle, and soundness of will, but also that the various elements of one's life and thought are integrated, or a uni-fied whole. A historian cannot, of course, get access to the inner reaches of a historical figure's heart, but after spending years exam-ining the record by and about Edwards, I can simply testify to the re-markable consistency of his life and thought. The private Edwards, at least from what he let anyone see, seems to be just the same as the public Edwards. He kept his theological priorities uppermost, as much so in relating to his family or preaching a sermon as when working countless hours on his notebooks or treatises in his study.

In social situations, he was little interested in small talk and always wanted to turn the conversation to weighty matters. The downside of these traits was that, especially to those who did not know him well, he appeared to be stiff, unsociable, and unrelievedly serious. Nonetheless, he was by all accounts amazingly consistent.

Despite his formality, Edwards was a passionate and affectionate man. His passions and his affections were driven by his theology, far more than for most people. In that integration of affections and intellect his life illustrated his teachings. Once he had experienced the gift of seeing the beauty of God's redemptive love in Christ at the very center of the universe, everything else became secondary. And only when one experienced the reality of God's redemptive love, he was convinced, could one truly love others as one ought. So whether in hazarding his life and family to minister to the Indians, or in risking excess in support of upstart young evangelists, or in writing letters to his children, he was driven by an overarching and passionate concern about a right relationship to God. Without it, eternity was a dark and terrifying prospect. With it, everything was as bright as day.

Suggestions for Further Reading

—◦◦◦—

Almost every topic discussed in this book is discussed at greater length in George Marsden, *Jonathan Edwards: A Life* (Yale University Press, 2003). The endnotes in that book will also lead the reader to many of the most helpful works on each subtopic.

By far the best resource is the Internet portal of the Jonathan Edwards Center at Yale University, http://edwards.yale.edu/. One can find all of Edwards's works at this site, including many sermons and notebooks not previously available. Under "Research Tools" one can find extensive bibliography on a large variety of subjects. Under "Teaching Tools" are suggestions for readings appropriate for high school or college levels or for pastoral or church group settings.

Edwards's own works are sometimes slow reading, since he does not economize on words but often states a point several ways in order to ensure complete clarity. His writing is therefore always lucidly clear, but his pace takes some getting used to. *A Jonathan Edwards Reader,* edited by John E. Smith, Harry S. Stout, and Kenneth P. Minkema (Yale University Press, 1995), provides an excellent selection of his basic works, including excerpts from his major treatises. Among his sermons, "A Divine and Supernatural Light," in that volume and other anthologies, is one of the most important and a good place to start. *The Sermons of Jonathan Edwards: A Reader,* edited by Wilson H. Kimnach, Kenneth P. Minkema, and Douglas A. Sweeney (Yale University Press, 1999), offers a fine selection. One of Edwards's most popular sermon series is *Charity and its Fruits,* available in many printed editions. C. Samuel Storms, *Signs of the Spirit: An Interpretation of Jonathan Edwards's "Religious Affections"* (Crossway Books, 2007), provides a readable paraphrase and interpretation of that classic text. Gerald R. McDermott, *Seeing God: Twelve Reliable Signs of True Spirituality* (InterVarsity Press, 1995), also offers an accessible updating of Edwards's argument regarding religious affections. John Piper, *God's Passion for His Glory: Living the Vision of Jonathan Edwards* (*with the Complete Text of* The End for Which God Created the World) (Crossway Books, 1998), presents one of Edwards's most important short treatises as spiritually inspiring today. John Piper and Justin Taylor, *A God Entranced Vision of All Things: The Legacy of Jonathan Edwards* (Crossway Books, 2004), offers essays reflecting on how various aspects of Edwards's outlook are still valuable for Christian believers.

Among the many fine books on Edwards's theology, particularly helpful places to start are Robert W. Jenson, *America's Theologian: A Recommendation of Jonathan Edwards* (Oxford University Press, 1988), and Michael McClymond, *Encounters with God: An Approach to the Theology of Jonathan Edwards* (Oxford University Press, 1998). Gerald R. McDermott, *One Holy and Happy Society: The Public Theology of Jonathan Edwards* (Penn State University Press, 1992), offers an introduction to Edwards's social thought. Robert E. Brown, *Jonathan Edwards and the Bible* (Indiana University Press, 2002), is a helpful introduction to that topic. For the context of the Great Awakening see Thomas S. Kidd, *The Great Awakening: The Roots of Evangelical Christianity in Colonial America* (Yale University Press, 2007). On George Whitefield, Harry S. Stout, *The Divine Dramatist: George Whitefield and the Rise of Modern Evangelicalism* (Eerdmans, 1991), and Frank Lambert, *"Pedlar in Divinity": George Whitefield and the Transatlantic Revivals* (Princeton University Press, 1994), are readable short biographies. *The Journal of Esther Edwards Burr, 1754-1757,* edited by Carol F. Carlsen and Laurie Crumpacker (Yale University Press, 1984), provides a fascinating window on the next generation.

Index

"JE" in the index refers to Jonathan Edwards. All works are by Edwards.